Acts

Dwelling in God's Word

Acts

Spirit-Empowered Witness to the Nations:
A Fifty-Day Devotional

GRAHAM JOSEPH HILL

Eagna Publishing • Sydney, Australia

ACTS

Spirit-Empowered Witness to the Nations: A Fifty-Day Devotional

Published by: Eagna Publishing (Sydney, Australia)
eagnapublishing@icloud.com
Cover and interior design: Graham Joseph Hill

paperback isbn: 978-1-7641791-4-0
ebook isbn: 978-1-7641791-5-7
version number 2025-11-06

NATIONAL
LIBRARY
CF AUSTRALIA
A catalogue record for this book is available from the National Library of Australia

Contents

Introduction

This devotional is part of a larger pilgrimage through Scripture, shepherded by Rev. Dr. Graham Joseph Hill, as he walks with readers from Genesis to Revelation. The Dwelling in God's Word series (both podcast and written reflections) invites you to discover how each book of the Bible speaks to the deep longings of the soul and the demands of our shared life in the world. It's not merely a reading plan; it's a sacred journey of formation and transformation. Here, the biblical narrative meets everyday discipleship in prayerful and practical ways.

The Acts of the Apostles burns with Spirit-fire and holy imagination. It's a book for the weary who long for renewal, for the timid who crave courage, for the scattered who yearn for belonging. Acts begins not with human plans but with the Spirit's wind, sweeping frightened disciples into a new creation. What unfolds is the story of God breathing life into a people who would bear witness in word, deed, and love, even when it cost them everything.

Here, prayer becomes power, prisons become pulpits, and strangers become family. Communities are formed around shared bread, shared burdens, and shared mission. The gospel breaks down walls of hostility, crossing languages, cultures, and empires, declaring that no heart, no home, no nation is beyond the reach of grace. Acts isn't a tale of perfect saints but of ordinary people made radiant by the presence of the risen Christ.

From Pentecost's flame to Paul's final breath, Acts invites us into the adventure of the Spirit: a life where chains fall, idols crumble, and the wounded are healed in Jesus's name. This is the story of the unstoppable gospel, the Spirit poured out on all flesh, the birth of a people whose hope can never be silenced. At its heart is the same invitation that still reaches us now: to open ourselves to the Spirit, to witness with our lives, and to join the incredible story of love that won't end.

This devotional is rooted in the richness of the biblical text and nourished by careful theological reflection. It invites you to sit with Scripture: slowly, reverently, attentively. Each entry draws you deeper into Acts, exposing overlooked treasures and summoning fresh faith. But this isn't just about knowing more. It's about living differently. As you journey through these pages, you'll be challenged to embrace justice, embody mercy, cultivate humility, and become a participant in the reconciling mission of God.

These reflections don't avoid hard questions or flatten the text into sentiment. They dare to wrestle. To pray. To imagine. And they call you to more than contemplation. They invite you to action: to live the lessons of Acts in your neighborhood, your body, your workplace, your church.

As you immerse yourself in this devotional, may your theology deepen, your heart soften, and your hands be ready to serve. May these fifty days in Acts stir something courageous in you: a longing to see and be seen by the living Christ.

How to Use This Devotional:

1. This book leads you through Acts in fifty short devotions.

2. You're encouraged to pair this with the companion podcast: https://grahamjosephhill.com/devotions.

3. Each day, you're invited to:

a. Read the passage slowly, letting it read you.

b. Sit with the day's devotion and let its truths sink deep.

c. Pray honestly and vulnerably, into the text.

2

d. Discern one concrete action in response.

Whether you read alone, with family, or within a community, this journey through Acts will shape your heart and stretch your faith. Come ready to be changed.

Day 1: The Ascending Christ and the Sending Spirit

Reading: Acts 1:1–11

The story of Acts begins not with the disciples' strength, but with their waiting. Luke reminds us that the risen Jesus spent forty days with them: teaching, breaking bread, showing wounds, giving many convincing proofs that he was alive, and speaking of the kingdom of God. The work of salvation is complete, but the work of witness and Spirit-empowerment has just begun.

The disciples ask what we might have asked too: "Lord, is this the time you will restore the kingdom to Israel?" They want clarity, control, and closure. They still see him as a Messiah with a mission limited primarily to Israel and its restoration. But Jesus doesn't give them a timetable. Instead, he promises power: "You'll receive the Holy Spirit, and you'll be my witnesses." The kingdom isn't about calendars but about calling. Creator God has set times and dates by divine authority, and our role is to follow and serve God's glory and mission, not become experts in God's timing.

Notice the scope of the calling God gives us, as witnesses of the crucified and resurrected Christ: "In Jerusalem, in all Judea and Samaria, and to the ends of the earth." The Spirit will push them outward, past familiarity, past prejudice, and past safety. The gospel won't be contained by geography, language, institution, nation, or culture. This is a mission that stretches as wide as creation and as deep as time.

Then comes the ascension. Jesus is lifted up, a cloud concealing him from their sight. It's not escape but enthronement. The one who stooped to wash feet, who bore the cross, who broke open the grave, who identified with us in our humanity, now takes his seat at the right hand of God. His authority is universal, his reign unshakable, his kingdom eternal.

And yet, the disciples stand staring at the sky. Their eyes are fixed upward, their hearts confused. Two messengers break the spell: "Why do you stand looking up toward heaven? This Jesus will come again." In other words: Stop gazing into the clouds; start preparing for the Spirit. The mission is ahead, not above. Jesus won't be gone forever; his Spirit will empower you, and he'll return from heaven in glory.

This passage speaks to us with piercing relevance. We, too, want timetables and certainty. We want God to fix the world according to our schedule. But Jesus redirects us: the kingdom comes not by our control, but by the power of the Spirit. The question isn't "when will it happen?" The question is "how will we witness in the meantime?"

This passage also warns us against a faith that only looks heavenward. Yes, our hope is anchored in Christ's return. But until that day, we're called into the world: to testify, to embody love, to cross boundaries for the sake of the gospel, to endure suffering and persecution, and to point others to the crucified and resurrected Christ Jesus. Ascension isn't abandonment; it's commissioning. The risen Christ reigns, and the Spirit empowers, so that the church can carry his presence into every place of exile, hunger, and longing.

The story of Acts begins here, with waiting, with promise, with eyes lifted but feet soon to move. And our story, too, starts again each day with this same invitation: Receive the Spirit. Bear witness to Jesus crucified and risen. Trust in God's providence and timing. Live between ascension and return with courage and hope.

Guiding Truth: The ascended Christ reigns, and the Spirit empowers us to be witnesses of his kingdom to the ends of the earth.

5

Reflection: Where am I more concerned with timetables than with witness? How is the Spirit calling me to cross boundaries for the sake of the gospel?

Prayer: Risen and ascended Lord, turn my eyes from speculation to mission. Breathe your Spirit into my weakness, that I may witness with courage and love. Send me outward, to embody your kingdom until you come again. Amen.

Day 2: Waiting in the Upper Room

Reading: Acts 1:12–26

After the ascension, the disciples return to Jerusalem. They don't scatter or rush into action; they wait. The upper room becomes their sanctuary. There, the eleven gather with women, with Mary, the mother of Jesus, and with his brothers. Already, the shape of the new community is taking form: no longer just a band of men, but a family of believers united in prayer.

This waiting isn't idle. It's a posture of expectation. Jesus had promised the Spirit, and now they hold still until heaven breathes. Prayer becomes their lifeline, binding them together as they prepare for what they can't yet imagine.

Amid this waiting, Peter rises to speak. They must face the loss of Judas. His betrayal and death leave a wound in the community and a gap in their number. But rather than pretending it never happened, they name it. They bring the pain into the light of Scripture. They acknowledge the brokenness, the tragedy, and the need for healing.

Then they act. They discern that another must take Judas's place: a witness to the resurrection, one who had been with them from the beginning. Two names are put forward: Joseph, also known as Barsabbas, and Matthias. They pray, asking God to show who has been chosen. Then they cast lots, and Matthias was numbered among the twelve.

This moment is rich with significance. The disciples don't rush ahead in their own wisdom, nor do they freeze in paralysis. They pray, they discern, they act. Their trust isn't in luck but in God's sovereignty. Casting lots becomes a way of surrendering control, a declaration that this mission belongs not to them but to God.

This passage holds profound wisdom. Too often, we're tempted to rush into activity without prayer, or to pray without ever acting. The early church models a third way: prayerful action and active prayer. They hold grief and hope together, naming what's broken while stepping into what God is building.

The waiting in the upper room is also a reminder that mission begins not with strength but with dependence. The Spirit hasn't yet come, but already their posture is shaped by expectancy. The church is born not in power plays or strategies but in prayerful trust.

This text invites us to examine our own upper rooms: those spaces where we wait, grieve, pray, and prepare for the future. It calls us to face the wounds in our communities with honesty, to seek God's guidance in our decisions, and to trust that even in our uncertainty, God is moving forward with both our stories and God's.

Guiding Truth: The church is birthed through prayerful waiting, honest lament, and trusting God to guide every step of its mission.

Reflection: What wounds in my life or community need to be named in prayer rather than hidden? How can I practice prayerful discernment instead of rushing ahead or stalling in fear?

Prayer: Faithful God, teach me to wait with hope. Please help me to hold grief and trust together. Guide my steps in discernment, that my choices may honor your wisdom and not my own. Make me ready for the Spirit's breath. Amen.

Day 3: The Spirit at Pentecost

Reading: Acts 2:1–13

The story of Pentecost is one of the defining stories and moments in the history of the church. The disciples were all together in one place. Waiting. Praying. Listening. Suddenly, the silence was broken by a sound from heaven like a rushing wind. It filled the house, spilling into every corner. Tongues of fire rested on each one, and they began to speak in languages not their own. The Spirit had come.

This is no private experience, no hidden ecstasy. The Spirit propels them outward. The noise gathers a crowd, pilgrims from every nation under heaven. Each one hears the disciples speaking in their own tongue. The message isn't confined to one culture or language but is made accessible to all. The gospel refuses to be bound by borders. Since the creation of the world, God has been moving to redeem and restore all of humanity and creation, and Pentecost is another demonstration of God's heart and mission.

The crowd is bewildered, astonished. Some are moved to wonder: "What does this mean?" Others sneer: "They're filled with new wine." Such is the way whenever the Spirit disrupts the ordinary: some hearts awaken, others harden, and others mock.

Pentecost isn't just about power; it's about reversal. At Babel, language was divided and scattered. At Pentecost, language unites and gathers. God's mission isn't to erase difference but to speak through it, weaving diversity into harmony. The Spirit affirms every culture, every tongue, every people, declaring that all are invited to hear and belong.

9

The fire that rests on each disciple also signals something profound. The Spirit doesn't anoint just the leaders or the outspoken, but all. Men and women, the bold and the hesitant, the Jew and the Gentile, the wealthy and those in poverty, the known and the overlooked: all carry the flame. This is the democratization of the Spirit. Every believer becomes a vessel of divine presence, every life a testimony.

For our spiritual lives, Pentecost is both comfort and disruption. Comfort, because it reminds us that God's Spirit dwells with us, empowering ordinary people to speak extraordinary truth. Disruption, because the Spirit won't let us remain turned inward. We're propelled into the streets of our world, called to speak God's wonders in ways others can understand. May the Spirit always comfort and disrupt us, soothe and disturb us, and give us peace and propel us into God's mission.

In a fractured age where division runs deep, this passage challenges us to reflect on our own perspectives. Do we believe that God's Spirit still unites across boundaries? Do we trust that the gospel can still be heard in every language, not just ours? Do we acknowledge God's presence among peoples, politics, ethnicities, cultures, traditions, and languages not our own? Pentecost calls us to humility, to listen as much as we speak, to celebrate the Spirit's work in places we least expect.

Some will mock. Some will grow hard. Some will persecute. Some will dismiss. But others will ask, "What does this mean?" That question remains at the heart of Pentecost. It's the question of those hungry for God, those startled by grace, those ready to hear the gospel in their own tongue. And it's the question the church must always be prepared to answer not with arrogance, but with the witness of Spirit-filled lives.

Guiding Truth: Pentecost shows us that the Spirit empowers all believers, unites them across differences, and propels them into witness for the sake of the world.

Reflection: How am I listening for the Spirit's voice across languages, cultures, politics, classes, genders, ethnicities, and experiences not my own? Where is the Spirit disrupting my comfort to send me outward in witness?

Prayer: Spirit of fire, rush through my life. Burn away fear. Give me words of truth in the language of love. Unite what is divided and send me to bear witness to your wonders in every place you call me. Amen.

Day 4: Courage to Rise and Speak

Reading: Acts 2:14–36

The Spirit has come with fire and wind. The crowd is buzzing with confusion: some are amazed, while others mock. Into the noise, Peter rises. Not the Peter of denial, but the Peter restored by grace, emboldened by the Spirit. He lifts his voice and speaks from his heart, drawing on his knowledge of Jesus Christ and the words of the Hebrew Bible.

Peter anchors the moment in prophecy. "This is what was spoken through the prophet Joel." The Spirit has been poured out on all flesh: sons and daughters, young and old, enslaved people and free, all experience the power and presence of God. The boundaries of privilege have collapsed, as God makes one new people for God's self. Revelation is no longer reserved for the few; the future is no longer locked in the hands of the powerful. God's Spirit fills every generation, every class, every gender, every ethnicity, every language, every culture, and every voice. This isn't just renewal; it's revolution.

Peter proclaims Jesus of Nazareth: the one attested by miracles, crucified by human hands, and raised to life by God. Peter doesn't soften the indictment: "This Jesus, whom you crucified, God has made both Lord and Messiah." The cross isn't an accident of politics; it's the revelation of human violence and divine love, justice, and mercy colliding.

But resurrection overturns it all. Death couldn't hold him. Peter calls upon the Psalms: "You won't abandon my soul to Hades or let your Holy One see corruption." The ancient song finds its fulfillment here, in the empty tomb, in the risen Lord who now reigns at God's right hand.

Peter's sermon climaxes not with abstract doctrine but with a living claim: Jesus is Lord and Messiah. The empire proclaimed Caesar as lord; religion sought to protect its systems; fear demanded silence. But Peter, once trembling, now declares boldly: the crucified one is sovereign over all. Jesus Christ, whom the prophets and scriptures foretold, has been crucified by people and raised to life by God, and now rules and reigns as Lord and Messiah over all rulers, powers, creation, Israel, and humanity.

This passage is both a historical proclamation and a present challenge. It reminds us that the gospel isn't polite advice; it's disruptive truth. It confronts injustice, unmasks violence, and insists that love has the last word. To proclaim Jesus as Lord is to say that no other power (political, economic, ideological, or cultural) holds ultimate allegiance.

Peter's sermon is a call to Spirit-filled witness. God doesn't ask us to be eloquent or relevant, but faithful and truthful. The Spirit takes ordinary words and infuses them with power. We need only stand, as Peter did, and bear witness to what God has done in Christ.

And like Peter, we must anchor our proclamation in both Scripture and Spirit, in both honesty about human failure and confidence in divine triumph. We aren't spectators of Pentecost but participants in its ongoing fire. The same Spirit that filled Peter fills us, too.

The first sermon concludes with a resounding affirmation: Jesus is Lord. Every sermon since must echo that truth, not as an empty formula but as the heartbeat of a new creation.

Guiding Truth: The Spirit empowers us to proclaim Jesus as Lord (boldly, inclusively, and truthfully) in a world still grasping for other lords.

Reflection: What powers or allegiances compete with my confession that Jesus is Lord? How is the Spirit inviting me to witness more boldly, even when fear or ridicule threatens?

Prayer: Spirit of truth, give me courage like Peter to rise and speak. Let my words be filled with your fire and my life with your witness. Let my heart worship and adore Jesus as Lord, and proclaim him crucified and risen in word, integrity, sign, and deed. May I confess with boldness that Jesus is Lord and live as if no other power can claim me. Amen.

Day 5: Cut to the Heart

Reading: Acts 2:37–41

Peter's Spirit-filled sermon falls like fire into the crowd. He has proclaimed Jesus crucified and risen, named him Lord and Messiah. The words pierce deeper than argument. "When they heard this, they were cut to the heart." This is the work of the Spirit: truth striking inward, conviction not as condemnation but as awakening.

They cry out: "Brothers, what shall we do?" It's the right question when the gospel is heard. Not what shall we think? Not how shall we explain? But what shall we do? The gospel demands a response. It doesn't leave us as we are.

Peter answers with simplicity and urgency: "Repent and be baptized, every one of you, in the name of Jesus Christ for the forgiveness of sins, and you'll receive the gift of the Holy Spirit." Repentance is more than remorse. It's a turning, a reorientation of life, a surrender of allegiance, a step into new creation. Baptism seals this turning, marking us not with shame but with forgiveness, not with exclusion but with belonging. And the Spirit isn't withheld from a chosen few: it's promised to all, to generations yet unborn, to those near and those far.

The crowd that once shouted for crucifixion now receives the invitation to life. This is the scandal of grace: that even those complicit in violence are offered forgiveness, that even those who mocked the Messiah are now welcomed into his kingdom. Grace doesn't erase the truth of our failure: it transforms it.

15

Peter presses the call further: "Save yourselves from this corrupt generation." Not escape, but resistance. To enter Christ's kingdom is to step out of the stream of destructive patterns, to reject the systems of fear and domination, to live as an alternative people marked by the Spirit.

And the response is astonishing. About three thousand are baptized that day. The church is born not in quiet strategy but in public repentance, not in carefully curated programs but in Spirit-driven transformation. The movement begins not with power but with pierced hearts and washed bodies.

This passage is both a mirror and an invitation. Do we allow ourselves to be cut to the heart by the gospel? Too often, we seek comfort over conviction, explanation over transformation. Yet the Spirit still speaks, still exposes, still calls us to turn and live.

It also reminds us that baptism isn't a private ritual but a public declaration of belonging. To be baptized is to step into a story larger than ourselves, to receive forgiveness, to embody new life, and to become a dwelling place for the Spirit.

Pentecost shows us that the gospel isn't a theory to admire but a reality to enter. The question still stands: What shall we do?

Guiding Truth: The gospel cuts to the heart, calls us to repent, and welcomes us into forgiveness, baptism, and the gift of the Spirit.

Reflection: Where's the Spirit convicting me: not to shame me, but to awaken me to life? How does my baptism still call me to live as one forgiven, Spirit-filled, and sent?

Prayer: Spirit of conviction and grace, cut through my defenses. Turn my heart toward your way. Let repentance shape me, forgiveness free me, and your Spirit empower me to live as your witness in the world. Amen.

Day 6: A Community of Devotion and Delight

Reading: Acts 2:42–47

Pentecost doesn't end with fire and preaching. It spills into daily life. The Spirit who filled individuals now forms a people. Luke describes a rhythm, a pattern, a way of being together that embodies resurrection in ordinary practices.

"They devoted themselves to the apostles' teaching and fellowship, to the breaking of bread and the prayers." Devotion is the keyword. This isn't casual interest or occasional attendance; it's wholehearted commitment. Teaching shapes their minds. Fellowship binds their lives. Breaking bread nourishes body and soul. Prayer roots them in God. It's a way of life, not a Sunday event.

"And awe came upon everyone, because many wonders and signs were being done through the apostles." This awe isn't entertainment but reverence. Miracles confirm that God's presence dwells in their midst. Awe is the proper response when heaven brushes against earth.

"All who believed were together and had all things in common." Here's the scandal of Pentecost: generosity without calculation. They sold their possessions and distributed them to anyone who had need. This isn't forced redistribution but Spirit-driven love. Possessions become tools of mercy rather than trophies of status. In a culture obsessed with accumulation, the Spirit gives birth to a community of sharing.

"Day by day, as they spent much time together in the temple, they broke bread at home and ate their food with glad and generous hearts." Joy pulses through their life together. Worship isn't confined to sacred buildings but spills into homes, kitchens, and tables. Gratitude and generosity are inseparable. The Spirit makes them both reverent in prayer and exuberant in fellowship.

"Praising God and having the goodwill of all the people." Their life together becomes a witness. Outsiders look in and see not fear or exclusion, but joy, generosity, and worship. The church's credibility isn't in its arguments but in its life: ordinary people living extraordinary love.

"And day by day the Lord added to their number those who were being saved." Growth isn't a result of marketing but of witness. God adds to the church as the Spirit's presence radiates through their practices. Salvation isn't a one-time decision, but a communal way of living that draws others in.

This story is a mirror. What does devotion look like in our communities? Do our tables carry the fragrance of joy? Do our resources serve only ourselves, or are they shared for the sake of others? Do outsiders see in us a life so generous, so rooted in love, that it awakens longing?

Acts 2:42–47 isn't nostalgia for a perfect past; it's a vision for Spirit-shaped life here and now. The Spirit who formed them is the Spirit who forms us. The invitation remains: to devote ourselves, to share generously, to eat with glad hearts, to live as signs of God's kingdom in the world.

Guiding Truth: The Spirit creates a community devoted to teaching, fellowship, generosity, joy, and witness: a foretaste of God's kingdom.

Reflection: What rhythms of devotion shape my daily life with God and others? How can I practice generosity and joy so that my life together with others becomes a witness to Christ?

Prayer: Spirit of community, knit us together in devotion, generosity, and joy. Let our tables be places of gladness, our prayers places of power, and our lives signs of your kingdom. Teach us to live as witnesses of your love in the world. Amen.

Day 7: Silver, Gold, and the Name of Jesus

Reading: Acts 3:1–10

Peter and John go to the temple at the hour of prayer. Their steps are steady, their routine familiar. Yet on this ordinary day, an extraordinary encounter awaits at the gate called Beautiful. A man, lame from birth, is carried there daily to beg. He knows the rhythms: prayer hours mean worshipers, and worshipers might give coins. Survival depends on the generosity of strangers.

He fixes his gaze on Peter and John, expecting the usual: alms, a small token, enough to keep him through another day. But Peter disrupts the pattern: "Look at us." The man does. And then comes the surprising word: "Silver and gold I don't have, but what I have I give you. In the name of Jesus Christ of Nazareth, rise up and walk."

This isn't charity; it's transformation. Peter doesn't offer a temporary solution but an encounter with resurrection power. He takes the man by the hand, lifts him up, and strength fills his feet and ankles. He leaps, walks, and enters the temple with them, praising God. The one excluded from worship, sitting at the margins, now strides into the very heart of prayer. The healed becomes a worshiper, the beggar becomes a witness.

The crowd is astonished. They recognize him as the man who once sat by the gate. His healing becomes a public sign, a testimony that the risen Christ is still at work through his followers.

When I was a child, my family often took summer holidays at Nelson Bay on the New South Wales coast, Australia. Every year, a Christian group would hold a beach mission in the area, and parents would send their children to participate in games, water sports, and Bible instruction. One of my most vivid memories is that camper walking around the caravan park belting out the song "Silver and Gold Have I None." I remember the words of the song making a great impression on me, as I imagined the biblical scene.

This passage reveals the nature of the Spirit's mission. It isn't about wealth or status, but about the power of Jesus's name to bring wholeness. The church isn't called to hoard resources or mimic the systems of empire, but to give what it has: the presence of Christ, the touch of compassion, the boldness of faith.

This story challenges and inspires. Too often, we settle for "silver and gold" solutions: charity that soothes without transforming, generosity that maintains the status quo. The Spirit calls us to more: to extend our hands, to name Jesus, to believe that healing is possible, not always as we expect, but always as a sign of God's kingdom breaking in.

It also asks us to look differently at those placed at the gates of our lives: the ones we pass daily, often without really seeing. Peter's words, "Look at us," remind us to engage, to notice, to treat others not as problems to solve but as people to encounter. The miracle begins with attention, with seeing and being seen.

At the Beautiful Gate, the gospel becomes visible: the excluded are included, the broken made whole, the forgotten restored to dignity, the beggar turned into a witness. This is what happens when the church dares to give not Silver or gold, but Jesus.

Guiding Truth: The Spirit calls us to offer not just resources but the transforming presence of Jesus, restoring dignity and bringing life where there was despair.

Reflection: Where am I offering "silver and gold" when God is inviting me to offer Christ himself? Who sits at the gates of my life waiting to be seen, lifted, and welcomed into worship?

Prayer: Jesus of Nazareth, open my eyes to those at the margins. Teach me to offer not just tokens of help, but your healing presence. Let my hand be an extension of your compassion, and may my life be a witness to your restorative power. Amen.

Day 8: The God Who Raises Up

Reading: Acts 3:11–26

The man who was once lame is now clinging to Peter and John, walking and leaping in the temple courts. Wonder ripples through the crowd. A miracle has unfolded before their eyes, and the people gather at Solomon's Portico, astonished.

Peter seizes the moment. He deflects their gaze: "Why do you stare at us as if by our own power or piety we made him walk?" The healing isn't a performance or a testimony to human greatness. It's the work of God through the name of Jesus.

He roots the miracle in the long story of Israel: the God of Abraham, Isaac, and Jacob has glorified his servant Jesus. The people handed him over to death; Pilate would have released him, but the crowd demanded a murderer instead. "You killed the Author of life," Peter says, "but God raised him from the dead." The bluntness is startling, but it's not condemnation; it's truth spoken for the sake of repentance.

The healing stands as evidence. Faith in the name of Jesus restored the man's body. What happened outside the gate is a living parable of what God desires for all: restoration, renewal, and new strength where there was only weakness.

Then Peter shifts: "I know you acted in ignorance, as did your leaders. But what God foretold through the prophets, that his Messiah would suffer, he has fulfilled. Repent, therefore, and turn back, that your sins may be wiped out, that times of refreshing may come from the presence of the Lord."

This isn't finger-pointing but an invitation. The call isn't to wallow in guilt but to turn toward life. Repentance is the doorway to forgiveness, and forgiveness opens into refreshment: a word that carries the sense of cool air, renewal, and Sabbath rest. The Spirit not only heals bodies but restores souls, families, and communities.

Peter reminds them of the promise: a prophet like Moses will come, and those who listen will live. He names the covenant with Abraham: "Through your offspring all peoples on earth will be blessed." In other words, what just happened in this temple court is part of God's ancient plan: restoration flowing outward, blessing spilling into every nation.

This passage reframes our understanding of the concept of witness. It isn't about claiming credit or showcasing power. It's about pointing away from ourselves and toward the risen Christ. It's about naming the truth of human brokenness and the greater reality of God's mercy.

It also challenges us to believe that repentance leads not to shame but to refreshment. Too often, we treat repentance as drudgery, but Peter portrays it as liberation: a turning that brings cool air to weary lungs and living water to parched souls.

The healing of one man becomes the proclamation of a kingdom. And that kingdom is still unfolding wherever lives are turned toward the One who raises.

Guiding Truth: The gospel calls us to repentance that leads to forgiveness and refreshment, always pointing to the God who raised Jesus from the dead.

Reflection: Where am I tempted to claim credit for what only Christ has done? How might repentance open space for times of refreshing in my life and community?

Prayer: God of resurrection, turn me from self-reliance to trust in your name. Lead me into repentance that heals, forgiveness that frees, and refreshment that renews. Let my life point not to me, but to Christ, who raises the broken to life. Amen.

Day 9: Boldness Before the Powers

Reading: Acts 4:1–22

The healing at the Beautiful Gate and Peter's sermon stir not only wonder but opposition. The temple authorities, priests, and Sadducees are "greatly disturbed" because Peter and John are proclaiming resurrection in Jesus. Resurrection threatens the status quo, disrupting the systems that rely on fear and control. So they arrest the apostles and haul them before the council.

Power confronts weakness, or so it seems. A group of untrained Galileans stands accused before the most educated, powerful, and prestigious leaders of their day. Yet when Peter speaks, it's not ignorance they hear but Spirit-filled boldness.

He names the heart of the gospel again: the man stands healed by the name of Jesus Christ of Nazareth, the one crucified and raised. He quotes Psalm 118: "The stone you builders rejected has become the cornerstone." The rejected one is now the foundation. And then the claim that rattles the hall: "There's salvation in no one else, for there's no other name under heaven given among mortals by which we must be saved."

The council is astonished. These men are ordinary, unschooled, pedestrian: yet their courage is undeniable. And then they recognize it: they'd been with Jesus. That's the difference. Their authority isn't in credentials but in companionship with Christ.

Unable to deny the miracle (the healed man is standing right there), the leaders command them to stop speaking in Jesus's name. But Peter and John refuse: "Whether it's right in God's sight to listen to you rather than to God, you must judge; for we can't keep from speaking about what we've seen and heard."

This is the heartbeat of witness: a compulsion to speak what can't be silenced. This desire to proclaim Christ isn't arrogance, nor defiance for its own sake, but fidelity to the truth they've encountered. They're ordinary people carrying extraordinary news, and no earthly power can muzzle it.

This passage is a call to Spirit-shaped courage. The world still pressures us into silence. We're told faith should stay private, that the gospel is too offensive, that truth should be muted for the sake of convenience. Yet Acts 4 reminds us: boldness isn't bravado but obedience and the overflow of having been with Jesus.

It also challenges how we measure authority. The council had education, power, and position. The apostles had wounds, witness, and the Spirit. Which has more lasting power? The testimony of resurrection outlives every human system.

And we see, too, that the evidence of the gospel isn't only in words but in lives transformed: the healed man standing beside them. Our boldness is strengthened when our lives, and the lives of those around us, bear visible witness to Christ's healing power.

Guiding Truth: True boldness doesn't come from status or skill, but from having been with Jesus and bearing witness to his resurrection.

Reflection: Where do I feel pressured to silence my witness, and how might the Spirit give me courage? What in my life bears visible evidence that I've been with Jesus?

Prayer: Risen Lord, fill me with your Spirit's boldness. Free me from fear of human power. Let my words and life testify that you're the cornerstone, the only name that saves. Keep me faithful to speak what I've seen and heard. Amen.

Day 10: Shaken and Sent

Reading: Acts 4:23–31

Released from the council, Peter and John return to their community. They don't come back with fear or with strategies for avoiding trouble, but with testimony. They recount what happened, how the rulers threatened them, and how the Spirit gave them the boldness to speak out. And the church responds not with panic but with prayer.

They lift their voices together, anchoring their prayer in Scripture: "Sovereign Lord, who made heaven and earth, the sea, and everything in them." Before addressing their crisis, they remember who God is: the Creator, the Sovereign, the One enthroned above every earthly power. Prayer begins not with our fear but with God's greatness.

They recall Psalm 2: "Why do the nations rage and the peoples plot in vain?" They see their own story mirrored in Scripture. Herod, Pilate, Gentiles, and Israel have conspired against the Lord's Anointed. Yet even in this conspiracy, God's purpose stands. What seems like defeat (the crucifixion) is the very means of redemption. The community views their opposition not as a failure of God's plan, but as its unfolding.

Then comes their request. They don't ask for safety or escape. They don't beg for their enemies to be destroyed. They pray for boldness. "Grant to your servants to speak your word with all confidence, while you stretch out your hand to heal, and signs and wonders are performed through the name of your holy servant Jesus."

This is remarkable. They know threats will come. They know persecution may rise. But instead of shrinking back, they ask for the courage to keep going. They understand that the mission isn't theirs to protect but God's to advance. Their task is to remain faithful, fearless, and full of the Spirit.

And God answers, not with comfort, but with power. The place where they're gathered is shaken. It's as if the ground itself testifies heaven's Spirit is present here. All are filled with the Holy Spirit, and they continue to speak the word of God with boldness. The prayer is answered immediately. Fear is replaced with fire.

This passage calls us to reimagine prayer. Too often, our prayers seek security, ease, or success. However, the early church shows us a better way: to pray for courage, faithfulness, and boldness to witness, even when it costs us. Pray for God's kingdom to advance through us, not for our comfort to increase around us.

It also reminds us that prayer is a communal experience. Their voices rise together. Unity fuels courage, and courage fuels witness. Alone we falter; together, shaken by the Spirit, we stand.

And perhaps this is what the church most needs now: not clever strategies or cultural influence, but Spirit-shaped boldness. A willingness to speak and live the gospel without fear, trusting that the God who made heaven and earth still shakes places and fills people with holy fire.

Guiding Truth: The Spirit answers the church's prayer for boldness with power, filling ordinary believers to speak and live the gospel without fear.

Reflection: Do my prayers seek safety, or do they seek boldness to remain faithful? How might I join others in prayer that shakes us out of fear and into mission?

Prayer: Sovereign Lord, shake my complacency. Please fill me with your Spirit. Grant me boldness to speak and live your word, even when it costs me. Let my life join with others as a witness to your kingdom's power and love. Amen.

Day 11: One Heart and One Soul

Reading: Acts 4:32–37

The Spirit who filled the believers with boldness now shapes their life together in extraordinary ways. Luke describes the community with breathtaking simplicity: "The whole group of those who believed were of one heart and soul." This isn't forced uniformity but Spirit-wrought unity. Their shared life is grounded not in ideology, culture, or preference, but in the resurrection of Jesus.

The apostles testify with incredible power to the risen Lord, and "great grace was upon them all." The grace that forgives sins also reshapes economics, possessions, and relationships. Grace isn't abstract; it becomes visible in the way they treat each other.

"There wasn't a needy person among them." These words echo Deuteronomy's vision for Israel, where God promised that if the people lived faithfully, there'd be no poor among them. Now, in the Spirit-filled community, that vision is realized. Believers sell land and houses, laying the proceeds at the apostles' feet, and distribution is made so that no one lacks.

This isn't coerced sharing or state-imposed redistribution. It's voluntary, joyful generosity springing from hearts transformed by resurrection. Those who once clutched possessions now release them for the sake of others. Property becomes provision. Wealth becomes witness.

Luke highlights Barnabas, a Levite from Cyprus, who sells a field and lays the money at the apostles' feet. His name means "son of encouragement," and his action encourages the whole community. His gift isn't only material; it's spiritual, embodying encouragement through generosity. Barnabas becomes a living sign of the Spirit's work: releasing resources, embodying unity, building up the body.

This passage presses us uncomfortably and beautifully. It challenges our culture of individualism and accumulation. The Spirit doesn't sanctify greed; the Spirit breaks its power. The resurrection creates a people who know that possessions are temporary but love is eternal. To be of one heart and soul means to see our resources as entrusted for the sake of others.

It also raises a question: What would it look like for there to be "no needy person" among us today? This isn't romantic nostalgia; it's a Spirit-born possibility. The same God who shook the place of prayer can shake loose our grip on wealth, teaching us to give, share, and trust.

Acts 4 reminds us that the Spirit's power isn't only for miracles and sermons but also for economics and daily life. Testimony about the resurrection is credible when matched by a community where generosity, equity, and love abound. The early church was compelling not only because of what it preached, but because of how it lived.

Guiding Truth: The Spirit creates a community marked by radical unity and generosity, where resurrection faith is embodied in shared life.

Reflection: How tightly am I holding to my possessions, and what might the Spirit be asking me to release? What practices of generosity could help make God's grace visible in my community?

Prayer: God of resurrection, loosen my grip on what I call mine. Make me generous with joy, bold with encouragement, and eager to share so that no one is left in need. Shape my life and community into a witness of your great grace. Amen.

33

Day 12: Holy Fear and Healing Power

Reading: Acts 5:1–16

The Spirit's work in the community is powerful, beautiful, and costly. Acts 4 ended with radical generosity, where possessions were sold so that no one was in need. But Acts 5 begins with a sobering contrast.

Ananias and Sapphira sell property but secretly hold back part of the proceeds while pretending to give the whole amount. Their sin isn't keeping some for themselves (Peter makes clear they were free to do as they wished) but lying to God and seeking honor without honesty. They wanted the appearance of generosity without the reality of surrender.

When Peter confronts Ananias, he falls dead. Later, Sapphira, unaware of what happened, repeats the deception and also dies. A great fear seizes the whole church. This isn't fear of random judgment but reverence for the holiness of God. The Spirit isn't to be manipulated for reputation or control. Hypocrisy corrodes community, and God protects the newborn church with sobering clarity.

The passage unsettles us, and it should. It reminds us that the Spirit's fire isn't tame. Grace isn't cheap. God desires integrity, not performance. The early church learns quickly that it can't mix resurrection power with deception. To be the dwelling place of God's Spirit means honesty matters, truth matters, holiness matters.

Yet the story doesn't end in fear alone. The following verses describe the Spirit's ongoing work, with signs and wonders abounding. The apostles gather in Solomon's Portico, and the people hold them in awe. More than ever, believers are added to the Lord, multitudes of men and women. The holiness that inspires fear also draws people to life.

The sick are carried into the streets, laid on mats and beds, hoping even Peter's shadow might fall on them. Crowds come from surrounding towns, bringing the sick and those tormented by impure spirits, and all of them are healed. Where hypocrisy brings death, authenticity brings life. Where deception fractures, truth restores. The Spirit's power is both purifying and healing, confronting sin and overflowing in compassion.

Acts 5 serves as both a warning and an invitation. It warns us against living for appearances: seeking honor without surrender, reputation without reality. God calls us to integrity, to live openly before the Spirit who sees all. Hypocrisy may impress people, but it grieves God.

It also invites us into the power of authentic community. When the church lives honestly, shares generously, and speaks truthfully, God's presence is palpable. Healing flows, lives are restored, the world takes notice. Holiness isn't about withdrawal from the world but about embodying God's truth and compassion within it.

Acts 5 calls us to reverence and boldness, integrity and compassion. The same Spirit who judged dishonesty also healed the multitudes. The Spirit is holy, and the Spirit is life.

Guiding Truth: The Spirit calls the church to integrity and holiness, so that its witness may overflow with healing and life.

Reflection: Where am I tempted to seek appearances rather than truth before God? How can I cultivate integrity so that my life becomes a channel for the Spirit's power and compassion?

Prayer: Holy Spirit, purify my heart. Expose my pretenses and make me whole. Fill me with honesty, reverence, and compassion, so that my life and community may bear witness to your holiness and healing love. Amen.

Day 13: Obedience Over Orders

Reading: Acts 5:17–42

The Spirit's power is spilling into the streets. The sick are healed, the oppressed set free, and multitudes are turning to Christ. But the joy of the people becomes the jealousy of the leaders. The high priest and Sadducees, filled with rage, arrest the apostles and throw them in prison.

Yet in the night, an angel of the Lord opens the doors. The command is simple and direct: "Go, stand in the temple courts and tell the people all about this new life." Freedom isn't given for escape but for witness. When morning comes, instead of hiding, the apostles are right back in the temple, proclaiming resurrection.

The authorities are bewildered. The jail is secure, the guards are in place, but the prisoners are gone. Soon, word comes: they're teaching again. The leaders drag them back, careful this time not to cause a riot. The high priest confronts them: "We gave you strict orders not to teach in this name. Yet you have filled Jerusalem with your teaching and are determined to make us guilty of this man's blood."

Peter and the apostles reply with words that have echoed through history: "We must obey God rather than human beings." This isn't defiance for its own sake; it's allegiance to the risen Christ. They proclaim again: Jesus, whom the leaders killed, has been exalted by God as Prince and Savior. Forgiveness and repentance flow from his name.

Furious, the council demands their execution. But a respected Pharisee, Gamaliel, counsels restraint. He reminds them of failed movements that have come and gone. If this is merely human, it'll collapse. "But if it's of God, you won't be able to overthrow them. You may even be found fighting against God." His words prevail, and the apostles are spared.

Yet they're flogged (a brutal punishment) and ordered again not to speak in the name of Jesus. But when they leave, they rejoice. Not because they enjoyed suffering, but because they were counted worthy to suffer for his name. And day after day, in the temple and at home, they never stop teaching and proclaiming Jesus as the Messiah.

This passage forces us to wrestle with obedience and courage. The apostles embody a faith that won't be silenced. They understand that obedience to God may mean defying human orders, enduring shame, and bearing wounds. Yet their joy is unshaken, because their lives are anchored in Christ's victory.

This is both a challenge and an encouragement. Challenge, because it calls us to resist the temptation of silence when truth is costly. Encouragement, because it reminds us that opposition doesn't defeat the gospel; it often strengthens it. The same Spirit who opened the prison doors strengthens our hearts to continue speaking, loving, and bearing witness, even when obedience leads to suffering.

Guiding Truth: The Spirit empowers us to obey God rather than human commands, even when faithfulness brings suffering.

Reflection: Where am I tempted to silence my witness out of fear of opposition? How might I find joy, like the apostles, in being counted worthy to suffer for Christ?

Prayer: God of freedom and courage, give me the strength to obey you above all else. Open the doors that fear has locked. Fill me with joy in the face of suffering and keep me faithful to proclaim Christ's name with boldness and love. Amen.

Day 14: Wisdom, Service, and the Face of an Angel

Reading: Acts 6:1–15

Growth brings beauty and tension. As the church multiplies, so do its challenges. A complaint arises: the Greek-speaking widows are being overlooked in the daily distribution of food. It's more than a logistical problem; it reveals cultural fault lines within the new community. The Spirit's work must be embodied not just in preaching and miracles, but in justice, equity, and care.

The apostles respond with wisdom. They don't ignore the concern, nor do they abandon their calling. They call the community together and say, "It's not right that we should neglect the word of God to wait on tables. Therefore, select seven people of good standing, full of the Spirit and wisdom, whom we may appoint to this task." This isn't a dismissal of service but a recognition of calling. The ministry of the word and the ministry of tables are both Spirit-filled and essential.

The community chooses seven, all with Greek names, ensuring that those previously marginalized are now represented in leadership. Stephen, Philip, Prochorus, Nicanor, Timon, Parmenas, and Nicolaus are set apart through prayer and the laying on of hands. The Spirit's solution to division isn't suppression but inclusion. Leadership expands, responsibility is shared, and the witness of the church grows stronger.

The result? "The word of God continued to spread; the number of disciples increased greatly in Jerusalem, and a great many priests became obedient to the faith." When the church practices justice and shares leadership, its witness gains credibility and power. Equity is part of mission.

Stephen, one of the seven, quickly emerges as a Spirit-filled witness. Full of grace and power, he performs wonders among the people. Opposition rises from members of the Synagogue of the Freedmen, who argue with him but can't withstand the wisdom and Spirit with which he speaks.

False accusations follow. Stephen is dragged before the council, accused of speaking against the temple and the law. The very systems that crucified Jesus are at work again, seeking to silence truth. Yet as charges are hurled, Stephen's face is described as that of an angel. In the midst of hostility, he radiates peace. The Spirit's presence is visible even in his countenance.

Acts 6 is a call to integrity in both structure and spirit. It challenges us to confront inequities in our communities honestly and to allow the Spirit to guide us toward creative, inclusive solutions. It reminds us that service and proclamation aren't competing callings but complementary streams of one mission. And it calls us to bear witness with courage, even when misunderstood or opposed, trusting that the Spirit who gives wisdom also gives peace.

Guiding Truth: The Spirit calls the church to shared leadership, equitable care, and courageous witness, shining with wisdom and grace even in the face of opposition.

Reflection: Where are inequities in my community that the Spirit may be inviting me to address with courage and creativity? How can I embody both service and bold witness in the places God has placed me?

Prayer: Spirit of wisdom and grace, teach me to serve with justice and to speak with courage. Make my life radiant with your presence, so that even in opposition, others glimpse the peace of Christ in me. Amen.

Day 15: A Story That Confronts

Reading: Acts 7:1–53

Stephen, accused of blasphemy, stands before the council. Instead of defending himself with clever arguments, he tells a story: the story of God's people. From Abraham's call to Joseph's trials, from Moses in Egypt to David and Solomon, Stephen traces the long arc of Israel's history. It's a history of promise and presence, but also of resistance and rejection.

Abraham was called to go, to trust without knowing where. Joseph was betrayed by his brothers, yet God was with him in prison and exalted him in Egypt. Moses was chosen to deliver, yet his people doubted him, turning back to Egypt in their hearts. The prophets spoke with fire, but their words were ignored again and again. Stephen's message is clear: God has always been faithful, but God's people have always resisted.

He points to the tabernacle and the temple, reminders that God dwells with the people. Yet even here, he warns against reducing God to a building or a system. The Most High doesn't live in houses made by human hands. The living God can't be contained, controlled, or manipulated.

Then Stephen turns from history to the present. His voice sharpens: "You stiff-necked people, uncircumcised in heart and ears, you always resist the Holy Spirit! As your ancestors did, so do you. Which of the prophets did your ancestors not persecute? They killed those who foretold the coming of the Righteous One, and now you have betrayed and murdered him."

It's not the response the council expected. Stephen doesn't plead for mercy. He doesn't try to save himself. He names the truth: the pattern of resistance continues, culminating in the rejection of Jesus. The same Spirit who spoke through Abraham, Joseph, Moses, and the prophets is still speaking, and still being resisted.

This passage is uncomfortable because it's meant to be. It confronts us with a sobering truth: it's possible to know the story of God and still resist the Spirit. It's possible to cling to tradition while missing God's living presence. It's possible to honor the prophets of the past while silencing the witnesses of the present.

Stephen's speech is both a mirror and an invitation. It asks: where do we resist the Spirit's leading in our time? Where are we stiff-necked, unwilling to release control? Where do we cling to buildings, systems, platforms, performance, or traditions as if God could be contained there?

And yet, Stephen's words are also hope-filled. They remind us that God's story is larger than our resistance. God's presence isn't bound to place or institution, but moves freely, raising witnesses, stretching out across history, calling us again to faithfulness.

Guiding Truth: God's story is one of faithful presence, but we're called to resist the temptation of stiff-necked hearts and to yield to the Spirit's living voice.

Reflection: Where might I be resisting the Spirit's prompting out of fear, pride, or comfort? How can I open myself to God's presence beyond the walls or systems I try to control?

Prayer: Living God, free me from a stiff neck and a closed heart. Open my ears to hear your Spirit today. Teach me to honor your story not only with my lips but with my life, yielding to your presence wherever you lead. Amen.

Day 16: Witness in Blood and Fire

Reading: Acts 7:54–8:3

Stephen's words pierce like arrows. The council, cut to the quick, grinds its teeth in rage. Yet even as fury swells around him, Stephen is filled with the Spirit. He gazes into heaven and sees glory: "Look, I see the heavens opened and the Son of Man standing at the right hand of God."

It's a breathtaking vision. Everywhere else in Scripture, the risen Christ is described as seated at God's right hand, enthroned in rest. But here, Christ stands. It's as if he rises to welcome his faithful witness, to honor his courage, to receive him home.

The council can't bear it. They rush at him, drag him out, and hurl stones. As rocks strike, Stephen prays: "Lord Jesus, receive my spirit." Then, echoing the words of his crucified Lord, he cries out: "Lord, don't hold this sin against them." His final breath is forgiveness. His dying act is mercy.

Saul, a young Pharisee, watches with approval. He guards the cloaks of those casting stones. Soon he'll become the church's fiercest persecutor, dragging men and women from their homes, ravaging the community of faith. The scattering begins as believers flee Jerusalem. What appears to be defeat becomes the seed of a mission. The gospel will now spread to Judea and Samaria, just as Jesus promised.

This passage confronts us with the cost of witness. Stephen doesn't die because he was unfaithful, but because he was faithful. His words and vision exposed hardened hearts, and truth is dangerous when power feels threatened. The first martyr of the church shows us that discipleship isn't always safe. But he also shows us that even in death, love triumphs. His prayers mirror Jesus's, embodying a kingdom where forgiveness is stronger than vengeance.

Stephen's death prompts the question of whether our faith is bold enough to face opposition, whether our love is deep enough to forgive even in pain, and whether our eyes are fixed enough on Christ to see glory when the world sees only shame.

It also reminds us that the Spirit is present in suffering. Stephen's vision isn't an escape from reality, but a revelation of reality's most profound truth: Jesus reigns, Jesus stands with his people, and no stone can silence the resurrection hope.

The scattering of the church is equally instructive. Persecution doesn't crush the gospel; it carries it further. What looked like loss became expansion. The blood of Stephen became seed for the mission. God redeems even violence for the spread of life.

Guiding Truth: The Spirit gives courage to bear witness, even in suffering, and turns persecution into seed for the gospel's growth.

Reflection: How might I fix my gaze on Christ so that fear doesn't consume me in times of trial? Where is God asking me to respond to hostility with forgiveness rather than retaliation?

Prayer: Risen Christ, stand with me when I'm afraid. Please fill me with your Spirit, that I may see your glory and forgive as you forgive. Use my life, even my wounds, as seed for your gospel's growth in the world. Amen.

Day 17: The Gospel Breaks Boundaries

Reading: Acts 8:4–25

Scattering could have silenced the church. Persecution forced believers from their homes, drove them from Jerusalem, and tore apart familiar rhythms. Yet wherever they went, they carried the gospel. What looked like defeat became a new beginning.

Philip goes to Samaria, a place thick with hostility and suspicion. Jews and Samaritans shared a tangled history of division, mistrust, violence, and prejudice. Yet this is precisely where the Spirit sends him. In the very place of division, Philip proclaims Christ. He heals the sick, drives out unclean spirits, and the city is filled with joy. The gospel doesn't reinforce barriers; it breaks them.

Among those who believe is Simon, a man known for magic. He had long amazed the people with his sorcery, earning their awe and even their devotion. But when he sees Philip's signs, he's captivated. He believes, is baptized, and stays close, astonished by the power of God.

When the apostles in Jerusalem hear that the Samaritans have received the word, Peter and John are sent. They pray for the new believers to receive the Spirit, laying hands upon them, and the Spirit falls upon them. The same Spirit who filled Jerusalem now fills Samaria. The same kingdom that began among the Jews now also embraces the Samaritans.

Simon, however, falters. Seeing the Spirit given through the apostles' hands, he offers money, hoping to buy the power. His old ways of thinking resurface: power as possession and influence as a commodity. Peter rebukes him sharply: "Your heart isn't right before God. Repent, for you thought you could obtain the gift of God with money." The Spirit is never a product to be purchased, only a gift to be received.

The story ends with the apostles testifying and returning to Jerusalem, proclaiming the gospel to Samaritan villages along the way. What began with persecution now blossoms into mission, spreading outward with unstoppable momentum.

This passage teaches us that hardship can scatter us into new mission fields. What we see as a loss, God often uses as a means of sending. It challenges us to cross boundaries of culture, prejudice, or division, proclaiming Christ in places we might least expect. The Spirit doesn't recognize our categories of insiders and outsiders.

It also warns us against treating God's power as a commodity. The Spirit is a gift, not possession; grace is received, not bought. Our calling isn't to control the Spirit but to be controlled by the Spirit.

Finally, it reminds us that the gospel produces joy. Samaria, long marked by tension, becomes a place of healing, freedom, and delight. The Spirit brings joy where there was estrangement, unity where there was suspicion.

Guiding Truth: The Spirit scatters us into new places, breaks down barriers, and reminds us that God's power is a gift, not possession.

Reflection: Where has hardship scattered me into new opportunities for witness? How might I cross boundaries of division to embody the joy of the gospel?

Prayer: Spirit of life, send me where I wouldn't have gone on my own. Break my boundaries, free me from control, and let me carry your gospel into places of division. Please fill me with joy and let that joy be contagious. Amen.

Day 18: On the Wilderness Road

Reading: Acts 8:26–40

After the revival in Samaria, the Spirit interrupts Philip's momentum with an unusual command: "Go south to the road (the desert road) that goes down from Jerusalem to Gaza." It must have seemed strange. Why leave a flourishing ministry for a barren road? Yet Philip obeys. The Spirit's call is often more about trust than logic, more about dependence than strategy, more about obedience than reason.

On that road, he meets an Ethiopian eunuch, a court official of great authority. He had traveled to Jerusalem to worship but, as a eunuch, would have been excluded from full participation in the temple. His identity placed him at the margins: he was a foreigner, an eunuch, and an outsider. Yet here he is, reading Isaiah aloud in his chariot, hungering for truth.

The Spirit nudges Philip: "Go to that chariot and stay near it." Philip runs alongside and hears the eunuch reading: "Like a sheep he was led to the slaughter." The eunuch asks the question that has echoed for centuries: "About whom does the prophet say this?"

Philip begins with that very passage and tells him the good news about Jesus, the suffering servant who brings life, the rejected one who brings welcome. Scripture opens into the gospel, and the gospel opens into grace.

As they travel, they come to a water source. The eunuch asks: "Look, here's water. What can stand in the way of my being baptized?" The question is rhetorical, bursting with hope. For so long, barriers had stood in his way: ethnicity, status, bodily difference. But in Christ, every barrier falls. Nothing prevents his baptism. Philip baptizes him on the spot. The outsider becomes embraced, the excluded becomes included, the seeker becomes a witness.

When they come up from the water, the Spirit suddenly takes Philip away. The eunuch goes on his way rejoicing, carrying the gospel back to his homeland. The good news leaps yet another boundary, moving further outward toward the ends of the earth.

This story is a vivid picture of God's boundary-breaking grace. It reminds us that the Spirit often calls us to unexpected places, wilderness roads where divine appointments await. It challenges us to listen, run, and engage when the Spirit nudges us toward those the world excludes.

It also confronts us with the eunuch's question: "What can stand in the way?" Too often, the church has placed obstacles where God has removed them: barriers of culture, gender, sexuality, language, class, or status. Acts 8 insists: nothing should stand in the way of those who believe. Baptism isn't guarded by human gatekeeping but opened by divine welcome.

The wilderness road becomes the place of revelation, joy, and inclusion. And it's often still in the wilderness, far from comfort, where the Spirit brings us to encounters that change lives and expand the kingdom.

Guiding Truth: The Spirit breaks down every barrier, sending us to wilderness roads where God's welcome embraces those long excluded.

Reflection: What "wilderness roads" might the Spirit be sending me to, even if they feel inconvenient or strange? Where have I allowed barriers to remain that the gospel has already torn down?

Prayer: Spirit who sends, give me courage to follow your nudges into wilderness places. Let me run toward those who are seeking and remove from me any barrier that blocks your welcome. Make my life a witness to your boundless embrace. Amen.

Day 19: Blinded to See

Saul is on the move, breathing threats, papers in hand, convinced he's serving God by eradicating the followers of Jesus. His zeal is lethal, his certainty unshakable. The road to Damascus is supposed to be a road of conquest. Instead, it becomes a road of revelation, encounter, collapse, and rebirth.

Suddenly, light blazes from heaven. Saul falls to the ground; his power stripped in an instant. A voice calls his name twice, "Saul, Saul, why do you persecute me?" The voice doesn't ask, "Why persecute my people?" but "Why persecute me?" To harm the church is to wound Jesus Christ. Saul realizes in one moment that the Jesus he thought was cursed is alive, enthroned, and united to his people.

Blinded, Saul must be led by the hand into Damascus. The vigorous persecutor becomes helpless, dependent. For three days, he neither eats nor drinks, a symbol of death before resurrection. The one who sought to destroy is now undone, stripped of sight, waiting for mercy.

Meanwhile, the Spirit speaks to a disciple named Ananias. The command is shocking: go to Saul and lay hands on him. Ananias protests: he knows Saul's reputation. To approach him is to risk betrayal or death. But the Spirit insists: "Go, for he's my chosen instrument to carry my name before Gentiles, kings, and the people of Israel. I'll show him how much he must suffer for my name."

Ananias obeys. He enters the house, lays hands on Saul, and calls him "Brother." The word itself is a miracle. Enemy becomes family. Scales fall from Saul's eyes, sight is restored, and he's baptized. The persecutor becomes an apostle, the destroyer becomes a servant, the enemy becomes a brother.

This passage confronts us with the disruptive grace of God. Saul isn't converted by argument or persuasion but by an encounter with the risen Christ. His zeal, his certainty, his violence: none of these can stand against divine love. Grace doesn't flatter or negotiate; it breaks, blinds, and remakes.

It also challenges us through Ananias. Obedience sometimes means approaching those we fear, calling "Brother" or "Sister" the very ones we would avoid. Ananias embodies the gospel's radical reconciliation: welcoming the enemy, trusting the Spirit, risking love. Without Ananias, Saul's story can't unfold. Without ordinary disciples obeying risky commands, the kingdom doesn't advance.

The story reminds us that conversion isn't the end, but the beginning. Saul is chosen not for comfort but for mission, to bear Christ's name and to suffer for it. To meet Jesus is to be sent.

Acts 9 offers hope and challenge. Hope, because no one (not even the fiercest opponent) lies beyond the reach of Christ's light. Challenge, because we too are called to obey, to embrace, to bear witness, even when it costs.

Guiding Truth: The risen Christ breaks into our certainties, blinds us to remake us, and calls us into mission through disruptive grace.

Reflection: Where am I clinging to certainty or power that Christ may need to shatter? Who might the Spirit be asking me to approach with courage and reconciliation, as Ananias did?

Prayer: Lord of light, break into my life as you did on the Damascus road. Shatter my pride, undo my false certainties, and send me where you will. I'm yours. Please teach me faithfulness through obedience, love, suffering, and trust. Please give me the courage to embrace those I fear and to live as a vessel of your disruptive grace. Amen.

Day 20: From Fear to Fellowship

Reading: Acts 9:20–31

Saul, freshly baptized and filled with the Spirit, doesn't wait long. Immediately, he begins proclaiming Jesus in the synagogues: "He is the Son of God." The transformation is astonishing. Saul has gone from persecutor to preacher, from denouncer to disciple, from terrorizer to transformed follower of Jesus Christ. Just days earlier, he was breathing threats; now he's breathing gospel. His life becomes the evidence: proof that the risen Christ not only forgives but remakes.

The people are bewildered. They say, "Isn't this the man who raised havoc in Jerusalem? Didn't he come here to arrest followers of this Way?" The irony is sharp. The hunter has become a witness. The persecutor now preaches the very name he once sought to erase. Once again, we see God transforming someone's heart and life, creating a new person for God's purposes and glory.

Saul grows in power and wisdom, confounding the Jews in Damascus by proving that Jesus is the Messiah. Yet his boldness provokes resistance. Plots to kill him form quickly, forcing his followers to lower him in a basket through an opening in the city wall. The one who once entered cities with authority now slips out hidden, vulnerable, threatened, and dependent.

Arriving in Jerusalem, Saul faces another barrier: fear from the disciples. They remember his reputation. They can't believe he's genuinely changed. Suspicion shadows him. It takes Barnabas, the "son of encouragement," to bridge the gap. Barnabas brings Saul to the apostles, recounting his vision of Christ and his bold preaching. Barnabas's advocacy turns fear into fellowship. Without his encouragement, Saul might have remained an outsider.

With trust established, Saul begins preaching in Jerusalem. Again, opposition rises. Hellenistic Jews argue with him, and soon another plot forms against his life. The disciples send him off to Tarsus for safety. What appears to be retreat is actually preparation. Saul will reemerge as Paul, carrying the gospel across the empire, as passionate as any other apostle to proclaim the Good News of the crucified and risen Jesus Christ.

The passage closes with a beautiful summary: "Then the church throughout Judea, Galilee, and Samaria enjoyed a time of peace and was strengthened. Living in the fear of the Lord and encouraged by the Holy Spirit, it increased in numbers." From chaos and persecution comes growth and peace. The Spirit guides, protects, and multiplies the church.

This passage reminds us that conversion isn't just a private transformation, but a public proclamation. Saul's new life immediately overflows with witness. Faith is meant to be declared, not hidden.

It also challenges us to be like Barnabas. Every community needs encouragers who see past reputation, who risk trust, who open doors for those others fear. Barnabas's role may seem quiet, but without him, Saul might never have been embraced. Encouragement is itself gospel work.

Finally, this passage teaches us that mission is costly. Plots, danger, and exile mark Saul's new life. To follow Christ is to embrace risk. Yet even in danger, the Spirit sustains the church. Fear doesn't have the last word: encouragement does.

Guiding Truth: Conversion births witness, encouragement builds community, and the Spirit turns fear into fellowship and growth.

Reflection: Who in my community needs a Barnabas: someone to advocate, trust, and encourage them into belonging? How can I proclaim Christ boldly, even when fear or opposition presses in?

Prayer: Spirit of encouragement, make me bold like Saul and gentle like Barnabas. Help me advocate for the outsider, proclaim Christ without fear, and trust your power to turn suspicion into fellowship and fear into peace. Remake and transform my life, that I may boldly and faithfully proclaim the Good News of the Messiah, in the power of the Spirit, to the glory of God. Amen.

Day 21: Rise and Live

Reading: Acts 9:32–43

As the gospel spreads through Judea, Galilee, and Samaria, Luke turns from Saul back to Peter. The same divine power flows through different vessels. Peter travels among the believers, and in Lydda, he meets Aeneas, a man who has been paralyzed and bedridden for eight years.

Peter speaks with Spirit-born simplicity: "Aeneas, Jesus Christ heals you. Get up and roll up your mat." Immediately, Aeneas rises. The healing is Christ's action: direct, present, and personal. News spreads, and many turn to the Lord.

Not far away in Joppa, a beloved disciple named Tabitha (or Dorcas) falls ill and dies. She's remembered for her kindness, generosity, and the garments she made for widows. Her community grieves deeply, sending for Peter in desperation.

When Peter arrives, he's surrounded by widows holding out the clothes she'd made: tangible testimonies of her love. It's a holy moment, saturated with sorrow and hope. Peter sends them out, kneels, and prays. Then he turns to her body and says, "Tabitha, get up." She opens her eyes, sees Peter, and sits up. He takes her hand and presents her alive.

The miracle floods Joppa with awe, and many believe in the Lord. The story is rich with echoes of Jesus' ministry: healing the paralyzed, raising the dead, and speaking simple yet powerful words. Peter is participating in the life of Christ, carrying forward the same Spirit of compassion and restoration.

This passage reveals the breadth of the Spirit's work. It isn't confined to preaching or teaching, but spills into healing, compassion, and raising the hopeless. The gospel is good news to believe and the power that makes all things new.

These stories also show the dignity of ordinary lives. Aeneas's healing restores both his body and his place in the community. Tabitha's resurrection honors the quiet, faithful service of a woman whose love clothed people experiencing poverty. In God's kingdom, acts of mercy are remembered, treasured, and used as testimony to the world.

We can trust that Jesus Christ still acts with power, healing brokenness and restoring life in both seen and unseen ways. This passage comforts us with the assurance that our ordinary faithfulness (our kindness, generosity, mercy, daily service) matters profoundly. God's Spirit breathes life through apostles and also through widows, garments, and communities bound together in love.

Peter's words to Aeneas and Tabitha echo into our lives: "Rise." The Spirit still calls the paralyzed to walk, the weary to hope, the broken to live. The kingdom is resurrection life, breaking into ordinary towns and people with extraordinary grace.

Guiding Truth: The risen Christ works through the Spirit to heal, restore, and even raise the dead, bringing resurrection life into ordinary places.

Reflection: Where do I need to hear Christ's word: "Rise"? How might I honor and embody the quiet, everyday acts of mercy that reveal God's kingdom?

Prayer: Living Christ, speak your word of life into my weariness. Heal what's broken, restore what's lost, and teach me to live faithfully in small acts of love. Make my life, like Tabitha's, a witness to your cruciform love and resurrection power. Amen.

Day 22: When the Spirit Breaks Our Boundaries

Reading: Acts 10:1–48

In Caesarea, a Roman centurion named Cornelius prays and gives generously to those experiencing poverty. He's devout, yet still an outsider to Israel's covenant. One afternoon, an angel instructs him to summon Peter. At the same time, in Joppa, Peter is on a rooftop praying. Hungry, he falls into a trance and sees a sheet descending from heaven, filled with animals that Jews considered unclean. A voice commands: "Get up, Peter. Kill and eat." Peter protests, but the voice replies: "What God has made clean, you mustn't call profane."

The vision comes three times. Peter is perplexed until Cornelius's messengers arrive. The Spirit says to Peter, "Don't hesitate to go with them, for I've sent them." The vision and the messengers collide: God is breaking down the wall between Jew and Gentile.

When Peter enters Cornelius's house, he admits the scandal: Jews don't associate with Gentiles, and they certainly don't commune and fellowship with them. But then he declares, "God has shown me that I shouldn't call anyone profane or unclean." Cornelius recounts his vision, and Peter begins to preach: God shows no favoritism but accepts all who fear God and do what's right. He proclaims Jesus's life, death, resurrection, and lordship over all.

As Peter speaks, the Spirit interrupts. The Holy Spirit falls on Cornelius and his household, and they begin speaking in tongues and praising God. The Jewish believers are astonished: the same gift given at Pentecost is now poured out on Gentiles. Peter, amazed, asks: "Can anyone withhold water for baptizing these people who have received the Holy Spirit just as we have?" They're baptized in the name of Jesus Christ, the first fruits of a mission that will carry the gospel to the ends of the earth and to all people, everywhere. God's mission is polycentric: from everyone to everyone, and from everyone to everywhere.

This passage is a watershed moment. The Spirit shatters centuries of division, prejudice, racism, religious superiority, and ritual boundaries. What was once unthinkable (Gentiles welcomed as equals in God's family) becomes undeniable through the Spirit's outpouring. The gospel isn't a tribal possession but a gift for all peoples.

As I read this story, I find it both liberating and unsettling. Perhaps you do, too. This account comforts us with the wideness of God's mercy: no one is excluded from the reach of Christ's love. But it also unsettles us, because it asks: whom have we labeled unclean? Whose houses would we hesitate to enter? Which groups do we hold prejudice against and avoid, shun, criticize, or exclude? Whose prayers, generosity, or longing for God have we overlooked?

Peter's transformation is as crucial as Cornelius's. The vision forces him to unlearn prejudice and embrace the scandal of grace. The Spirit does the same with us, pushing us out of our safe categories, confronting our hidden biases, and inviting us to see what God has already made clean.

Finally, Cornelius's household rejoices, Peter's heart expands, and the church is forever changed. When the Spirit breaks our boundaries, the kingdom comes nearer, our hearts expand, our lives become fuller, and our discipleship becomes more Christlike.

Guiding Truth: God shows no favoritism; the Spirit breaks down every barrier, welcoming all people into the family of Christ.

Reflection: Who in my life or community have I labeled "unclean," and how might the Spirit be calling me to see them differently? How can I open my life to the wideness of God's welcome without hesitation?

Prayer: Spirit of boundary-breaking love, expose my prejudices and widen my heart. Teach me to see no one as unclean, but all as beloved. Please help me to embrace those I'd usually avoid or exclude. Please soften my heart, open my life, and make me more like Jesus. Use me as a vessel of your welcome, that your kingdom may come in every household and every heart. Amen.

Day 23: When the Church Learns to Breathe Wider

Reading: Acts 11:1–30

News travels fast. By the time Peter returns to Jerusalem, word has already spread: he has entered the house of Gentiles and eaten with them. The Spirit has moved, but suspicion lingers. Old lines are hard to erase, even when God has already crossed them.

The believers confront Peter. Their question is blunt: "Why did you go into the house of uncircumcised men and eat with them?" They aren't celebrating the inclusion of Cornelius's household; they're worried about purity, tradition, and control. This is how communities often respond to change: with fear rather than joy.

But Peter doesn't argue. He tells the story. He recounts the vision of the sheet, the Spirit's command not to hesitate, Cornelius's prayer, the angel's message, and the Spirit falling on the Gentiles just as it did at Pentecost. He ends with a piercing question: "Who was I to think that I could stand in God's way?"

Silence follows. Then awe. Then worship. "So then, even to Gentiles God has granted repentance that leads to life." The church exhales, its lungs expanding. Grace is wider than they imagined.

The story shifts to Antioch. Persecution has scattered believers far beyond Jerusalem, and in Antioch, some begin speaking to Greeks as well as Jews. The Spirit blesses it, and many turn to the Lord. When Jerusalem hears, they send Barnabas to check it out. Barnabas sees what's happening and rejoices. He doesn't try to control it; he encourages it. True to his name, the son of encouragement sees grace and calls it good.

Barnabas then goes to find Saul, drawing him into the work. Together they teach in Antioch for a year, and it's here that believers are first called "Christians." It's not a label they claim for themselves: it's one others give, seeing that their lives are so Christ-shaped that no other name will do.

The chapter ends with famine looming. Prophets warn of hardship, and the disciples in Antioch respond with generosity. Each gives according to their ability, sending relief to Judea. This is what the Spirit does: expands vision outward, moves hearts to share, and binds communities across difference into one body of care.

What do we learn here? That the Spirit keeps pushing the church to breathe wider, to welcome those once excluded, to tell stories of God's surprising grace, to rejoice when life springs up in unexpected places. And we learn, too, that generosity is the natural fruit of grace. When God's love enlarges hearts, hands open.

The Spirit keeps asking us the same question Peter asked himself: Who are you to stand in God's way?

Guiding Truth: The Spirit widens the church's vision, teaching us to rejoice in God's welcome and to respond with generous love.

Reflection: Where might I be standing in God's way, clinging to old boundaries? How can I join the Spirit's work of encouragement and generosity today?

Prayer: God of wide mercy, stretch my heart to match your grace. Keep me from standing in your way. May I be quick to rejoice in the lives you touch, and eager to share what I've so that your church may thrive in love. Amen.

Day 24: Chains, Angels, and a Silenced Throne

Reading: Acts 12:1–25

The chapter opens in darkness. Herod, eager to please the powerful, stretches out his hand against the church. James, brother of John, is executed. Peter is seized and imprisoned, guarded by squads of soldiers. Violence sits on the throne, and the church seems vulnerable, exposed, fragile.

But Luke writes one of the most profound sentences in all of Acts: "But the church was earnestly praying to God for him." Herod has soldiers, swords, and authority. The church has faith, hope, and prayer. Christ's Spirit is with them. And heaven listens.

In the night, an angel of the Lord appears. Light fills the cell. Peter, chained between guards, is awakened: "Quick, get up!" The chains fall. The iron gate opens on its own. Peter walks into freedom, hardly believing it's real until the night air hits his face. Deliverance comes not through rebellion or strategy but through the hand of God, responding to the prayers of the saints.

Meanwhile, in a house packed with believers praying, Rhoda hears Peter knocking at the door. Overcome with joy, she leaves him standing at the door. The church, still praying for Peter's release, struggles to believe their prayer has already been answered. Faith is often like this: earnest yet slow to grasp the immediacy of God's intervention.

67

The scene then shifts. Herod, puffed up by flattery, sits on his throne. The people hail him as a god. He drinks in the praise, and in that moment, he is struck down. His own pride devours the one who wielded violence against the church. Kings fall, but "the word of God continued to spread and flourish."

This passage speaks to us in three ways. First, it reminds us of the power of prayer. The church, seemingly powerless, discovered that prayer is resistance: it's the refusal to concede the world to violence and empire. Second, it reminds us of God's deliverance. Chains fall not because of human ingenuity but because Christ is Lord over prison and gate. Third, it warns us of pride. Herod's death is a grim reminder that self-exaltation is a path to ruin.

For our spiritual lives, Acts 12 calls us to pray with persistence, to trust God's power even in impossible situations, and to live humbly, refusing the intoxicating allure of self-glory. It calls us to see in Peter's deliverance the deeper truth: Jesus is the one who breaks chains, opens gates, and silences thrones.

Guiding Truth: Prayer, humility, and trust in Christ's power overturn the oppression of rulers and the chains of empires and advance God's kingdom.

Reflection: Where am I tempted to rely on power or strategy rather than prayer and trust in God's Spirit? How might humility protect me from the price that blinds and destroys?

Prayer: Delivering Lord, teach me to pray with faith, to trust your power in the face of chains, and to walk humbly in your ways. Break my pride, release my fears, and let your word flourish in and through my life. Amen.

Day 25: Sent by the Spirit, Opposed by the World

Reading: Acts 13:1–12

In Antioch, a diverse community of prophets and teachers gathers in worship. They fast, they pray, they wait. Among them are Barnabas, Simeon, also known as Niger, Lucius of Cyrene, Manaen, and Saul: a blend of cultures and backgrounds, evidence that the Spirit creates unity from differences. While they worship, the Spirit speaks: "Set apart for me Barnabas and Saul for the work to which I've called them."

The church responds not with hesitation, but with more fasting and more prayer. Then they lay hands on them and send them out. Mission begins not with human strategy but with worshipful listening. To be sent is first to be still before God.

Barnabas and Saul, accompanied by John Mark, travel to Cyprus. There they proclaim the word in synagogues, sowing seeds of the kingdom. Soon, they meet resistance. In Paphos, a Jewish sorcerer named Elymas, advisor to the proconsul Sergius Paulus, opposes them, trying to turn the official away from the faith. The gospel is never proclaimed without challenge; every mission encounters powers that fear losing their grip.

But Saul, now called Paul, filled with the Spirit, confronts Elymas. His words are sharp: "You're a child of the devil and an enemy of everything right! You're full of deceit and trickery." It isn't anger, but discernment: Spirit-given clarity about what is at stake. Elymas is struck blind, stumbling in the very darkness he tried to spread.

The proconsul, witnessing both the power and the teaching, believes The gospel breaks into the heart of Roman authority, not by flattery or compromise, but by truth revealed through Spirit-filled courage.

This passage carries weight for our own discipleship. First, it reminds us that mission flows out of worship. Too often, we treat mission as an activity and worship as preparation, but here, worship is the birthplace of mission. When the church listens together for the Spirit's voice, direction comes.

Second, it warns us that opposition will rise wherever the gospel challenges entrenched power or deception. The way of Jesus exposes lies and lies fight back. The task of the church isn't to outwit the deceiver but to remain Spirit-filled and faithful, trusting that truth has power greater than trickery.

Finally, it calls us to courage. Paul didn't shrink back, and the Spirit honored his boldness. We, too, are called to confront what distorts, misleads, and blinds, whether in our own hearts or in the systems around us, not with cruelty, but with clarity born of love for the truth.

At the center of this story is Jesus, the one who still sends, still speaks, still overcomes deception with light. His Spirit leads the church outward, beyond boundaries, into contested spaces where grace meets resistance. And still, the word bears fruit.

Guiding Truth: Mission begins in worship, meets resistance in the world, and advances through Spirit-filled courage and truth.

Reflection: How can I create space in worship to hear the Spirit's direction for my life and community? Where is the Spirit calling me to confront deception with courage and clarity?

Prayer: Spirit of truth, root my mission in worship. Send me where you will and give me the courage to face resistance with love and boldness. Let my life, like Paul's, bear witness that your word is stronger than deception, your light brighter than any darkness. Amen.

Day 26: Good News for Jew and Gentile

Reading: Acts 13:13–52

Paul and Barnabas travel inland to Pisidian Antioch. On the Sabbath, they join the synagogue gathering. After the readings from the Law and the Prophets, the rulers invite them: "Brothers, if you have a word of exhortation for the people, please speak." Paul rises, gestures with his hand, and begins to tell the story. And what a story it is!

He recounts Israel's history: God chose the ancestors, delivered them from Egypt, sustained them in the wilderness, gave them land, raised judges and kings, and promised a Savior from David's line. That Savior is Jesus the Messiah. Paul proclaims his death at the hands of those in Jerusalem, his resurrection by the power of God, and the forgiveness of sins offered in his name. Through Jesus, Paul declares, everyone who believes is justified: a freedom the law of Moses couldn't provide.

The message stirs hearts. The people beg to hear more the next Sabbath. Many Jews and devout converts follow Paul and Barnabas, who urge them to continue in the grace of God. The following week, almost the whole city gathers. Crowds swell, and with them, opposition. Some of the Jewish leaders are filled with jealousy, contradicting and insulting Paul.

Paul and Barnabas respond with clarity: the message was first spoken to the Jewish people, but since many reject it, they'll turn to the Gentiles. Quoting Isaiah, they declare: "I've made you a light for the nations, that you may bring salvation to the ends of the earth." The Gentiles rejoice. They honor the word of the Lord, and many believe in it. The word spreads, even as persecution drives Paul and Barnabas out of the region.

The chapter closes with a paradox: the disciples are filled with joy and with the Holy Spirit, even amid rejection. Opposition can't quench the Spirit's fire. The mission widens, the word advances, and joy rises where faith is born.

This passage is a turning point. The gospel is proclaimed as the fulfillment of God's promises to Israel, yet it bursts beyond the boundaries of covenant history into the Gentile world. What begins in synagogue walls spills into the city streets. The Spirit insists that salvation is for all people.

For us, this story carries both encouragement and challenge. Encouragement, because it reminds us that God's promises are trustworthy: Jesus is the fulfillment of ancient hope, and his resurrection is the anchor of our faith. Challenge, because it asks us whether we're willing to embrace the wideness of God's mercy, even when it unsettles our boundaries.

It also teaches us about resilience. Paul and Barnabas don't stop when opposed; they redirect, obeying the Spirit's call to the nations. Joy and resistance often come together. The Spirit's presence doesn't guarantee ease, but it does guarantee life and hope wherever the word is welcomed.

Guiding Truth: The gospel fulfills God's promises to Israel and breaks open for all nations, bringing joy even in the face of resistance.

Reflection: How is the Spirit inviting me to widen my vision of who belongs in God's family? When opposition or rejection comes, how can I stay rooted in joy and resilience?

Prayer: God of promise and fulfillment, let your word take root in me. Please give me the courage to welcome the wideness of your mercy, resilience when opposed, and joy that flows from your Spirit's presence. Please fill me with the courage only you can provide. May my heart expand with your love, my mind rejoice in your truth, and my soul be filled with courage to proclaim Jesus Christ crucified, risen, and glorified. Send me as a light to reflect your salvation in the world. Amen.

Day 27: Speaking Boldly, Staying Faithful

Reading: Acts 14:1–7

Paul and Barnabas enter the synagogue in Iconium, and once again, they begin where they always start: with the word. They speak in such a way that many Jews and Greeks believe. The gospel breaks through, not solely because of eloquence, but because the Spirit animates their witness. Faith is born in hearts, crossing ethnic and cultural lines.

But belief is never the whole story. Opposition rises. Some refuse the message and stir up hostility, poisoning minds against the brothers. The mission is met not only with welcome but with resistance. This tension runs through Acts: the same word that brings life also provokes anger, fear, and division.

Paul and Barnabas don't flee. They remain "for a long time," speaking boldly for the Lord. Boldness here doesn't mean arrogance or recklessness; it means perseverance, courage, and trust that the truth is worth proclaiming even when contested. Their message is confirmed by signs and wonders, which serve as evidence that God's grace is active among them.

The city becomes divided, with some aligning with the apostles and others with their opponents. The gospel is disruptive; it refuses to remain neutral. Eventually, a plot to mistreat and stone them surfaces. This time, they discern it's right to leave, moving on to the surrounding region. They're bold but not reckless; faithful but not naïve. Their leaving isn't defeat but discernment. The mission continues.

This brief passage teaches us something vital about discipleship. Speaking the gospel faithfully will both draw people in and divide them. We can't expect the message of Christ's kingdom (one that exposes idols, confronts injustice, and offers grace that undermines pride) to be met with universal applause. The question isn't whether we'll face opposition, but whether we'll remain faithful when we do.

It also calls us to a particular kind of boldness. Boldness isn't shouting louder or winning arguments. Boldness is staying rooted in Christ when fear tempts us to silence. It's speaking truth with humility and clarity, trusting that God confirms the message in ways we can't orchestrate.

Finally, it reminds us that discernment is part of courage. There are times to stay and endure, and times to move on for the sake of the mission. Paul and Barnabas model a faith that listens to the Spirit, not pride, when deciding whether to stand or step away. Their courage isn't stubbornness; it's a matter of obedience.

At the center of this story is Jesus, the faithful witness who spoke truth even when opposed, who endured hostility with steadfast love, and who entrusted the outcome to God. To follow him is to live with that same boldness: humble, discerning, Spirit-filled, and resilient.

Guiding Truth: Faithful witness means boldness in speaking the gospel, discernment in opposition, and trust that God's Spirit confirms the message.

Reflection: Where am I tempted to be silent out of fear of rejection or division? How can I discern when to remain and when to move on in faithfulness to God's mission?

Prayer: Spirit of boldness, steady my heart in witness. Teach me to speak with humility and courage, to discern wisely in opposition, and to trust your power to confirm the gospel. Keep me faithful, wherever you send me. Amen.

Day 28: Healing, Misunderstanding, and the Cost of Witness

Reading: Acts 14:8–20

In Lystra, Paul notices a man crippled from birth, unable to walk. As Paul speaks, he sees something deeper: faith rising in the man's eyes. With a loud voice, Paul calls him to stand. The man leaps up, healed. A miracle bursts into public view, the kind of sign that can't be ignored. The God of Jesus and Israel has shown up in power, confirming God's compassion and Christ's gospel.

But the crowd misunderstands. They cry out in their own language, "The gods have come down to us in human form!" They call Barnabas Zeus and Paul Hermes. Priests bring bulls and garlands, preparing sacrifices. The miracle that was meant to point to the living God is twisted into idolatry.

Paul and Barnabas are horrified. They tear their clothes, rushing into the crowd, pleading: "Friends, why are you doing this? We're human like you. We bring you good news, that you should turn from these worthless things to the living God, who made heaven and earth and everything in them." They redirect the people, not to themselves, but to the Creator whose kindness is seen in rain, harvest, food, and joy. Still, their words barely restrain the crowd.

Then the scene turns violent. Opponents arrive from Antioch and Iconium, stirring hostility. The same crowd that wanted to worship Paul now stones him, dragging him outside the city, leaving him for dead. Idolatry and human whims are a volatile mix. But when the disciples gather around him, Paul rises and walks back into the city. The mission continues, marked by both miracles and scars.

This passage captures the complexity of Christian witness to Jesus Christ. First, it shows the power of God's Spirit working through frail human vessels. Healing is real. Lives are changed. But the same miracle that reveals truth can be misinterpreted, bent by cultural assumptions and human imagination. Even grace can be twisted into idolatry if people worship the gift instead of the Giver.

Second, it reminds us of the humility required in mission. Paul and Barnabas refuse glory. They don't accept the adulation of the crowd. They don't exploit misunderstanding for influence. They point away from themselves toward the Creator. Faithful ministry never builds an empire around personalities: it turns people toward the living God.

Finally, it speaks of resilience. Paul is stoned, left for dead, yet he rises. His strength isn't his own. He embodies the cruciform pattern of discipleship: suffering followed by resurrection power, weakness transformed into perseverance. This is the cost and the glory of following Jesus.

For us, the story poses a question: How do we respond when God's gifts in our lives are misunderstood or distorted? Do we deflect praise to God, or do we quietly absorb the glory? And when opposition comes (when the same voices that cheer one moment condemn the next), will we endure?

Jesus himself healed, redirected worship, and bore rejection. His way still calls us: to serve with humility, to point beyond ourselves, and to walk resiliently through both acclaim and hostility, trusting that the Spirit will raise us to stand again.

Guiding Truth: True witness points beyond ourselves to the living God and endures both misunderstanding and opposition with resilience.

Reflection: Where might I be tempted to receive glory that belongs to God alone? How is God calling me to endure misunderstanding or hostility for the sake of the gospel?

Prayer: Living God, keep me humble in witness, bold in truth, and resilient in suffering. Let every gift point beyond me to your glory. Strengthen me to rise when struck down, and to walk again in the way of Jesus. Amen.

Day 29: Strengthened Through Many Trials

Reading: Acts 14:21–28

After being beaten, rejected, and nearly killed, Paul and Barnabas continue their mission. In Derbe, they preach the good news, and many become disciples. Yet instead of moving on in triumph, they return to the very cities where they'd faced hostility: Lystra, Iconium, and Antioch. This is no accident. They recognize that disciples require more than mere conversion; they need strengthening, encouragement, and guidance to persevere in their faith.

Their message is honest: "We must go through many hardships to enter the kingdom of God." Not prosperity, not ease, but hardship. The way of Christ isn't an escape from suffering, but perseverance through it. The kingdom isn't built by avoiding pain but by enduring with perseverance, character, faith, hope, and love.

They appoint elders in every church, laying hands in prayer and fasting. Leadership is discerned in dependence on God, not based on popularity and charisma. These elders are entrusted to the Lord, the true shepherd of the flock.

From there, Paul and Barnabas travel back to the coast, sailing to Antioch, the church that first sent them out. They gather the believers and tell the story: how God opened the door of faith to the Gentiles. This is more than a mission report. It's testimony that the Spirit is fulfilling promises far bigger than any one community. Salvation is breaking boundaries. The kingdom is advancing. The mission belongs to God, and Paul and Barnabas, as God's servants and beloved children, as they pursue that mission.

This passage reminds us that discipleship is a path of risk-taking, obedience, and courage, not complacency, self-directedness, and comfort. Hardship is often the road by which the kingdom of God is entered. The Christian life doesn't promise escape from trouble, but rather presence in it: the presence of Christ, the presence of community, and the presence of Spirit-strength.

It also reminds us of the importance of leadership rooted in prayerful discernment. In an age obsessed with influence and visibility, the appointment of elders through fasting and prayer reveals a different approach. Authentic leadership is entrusted, not seized. It emerges from the Spirit's work, not ambition.

Finally, this passage lifts our vision beyond ourselves. Paul and Barnabas recount the opening of the door of faith to the Gentiles. Mission is always larger than our own story, our own community, and our own control. God is opening doors we don't see, inviting us to marvel, celebrate, and participate in the wideness of mercy.

At its heart, this story points us back to Jesus, the one who faced suffering, entrusted himself to the Father, and through his death and resurrection opened the door of life for all. To follow him is to walk the path of endurance, humility, and boundless joy in God's mission.

Guiding Truth: The kingdom advances through hardship, obedience, Spirit-shaped leadership, and the widening mercy and grace of God.

Reflection: How do I respond when faith leads me into hardship rather than ease? Where might God be opening doors of faith beyond my expectations or comfort?

Prayer: Christ Jesus, please strengthen me to endure hardship with faith and hope. Please teach me to trust in your Spirit's leading, to encourage others, and to rejoice when you open doors wider than I can imagine. May you keep me faithful to your mission, wherever it leads. Amen.

Day 30: The Council of Grace

Reading: Acts 15:1–35

Conflict erupts in the early church. Some believers insist that unless Gentile converts are circumcised according to the law of Moses, they can't be saved. What began as a movement of the Spirit and freedom is threatened by division and legalism. The apostles and elders gather in Jerusalem to wrestle with the question: what does it mean to belong to the people of God?

Peter stands and tells his story. God chose him to bring the gospel to Gentiles, and the Spirit came upon them just as on the Jews. "Why test God," he asks, "by placing a yoke on their necks that our ancestors nor we could bear? We believe it's through the grace of the Lord Jesus that we're saved, just as they are."

Paul and Barnabas then recount the signs and wonders God has done among the Gentiles through their ministry. Finally, James, leader of the Jerusalem church, offers discernment rooted in Scripture: the prophets had already foretold that God planned to include the nations. He concludes that Gentiles shouldn't be burdened with the full weight of the law but should abstain from practices tied to idolatry and immorality, for the sake of unity.

A letter is written and sent to the Gentile believers. It doesn't come with demands but with encouragement: "It seemed good to the Holy Spirit and to us not to burden you . . . " The church chooses grace over gatekeeping, inclusion over exclusion, unity over division. When the letter is read in Antioch, the people rejoice. Encouragement, not burden, becomes the fruit of discernment.

This passage reminds us that conflict in the church isn't new. What matters is how we respond: with listening, discernment, and a posture open to the Spirit's leading. The council models a community that refuses easy answers and seeks God together in humility.

Second, it centers salvation in grace. Belonging is about the gift of God in Jesus Christ, not cultural markers, religious legalities, or human effort. The church is called to resist every temptation to add conditions that the gospel itself doesn't place.

Finally, it calls us to unity that's Spirit-shaped. The decision is made to honor what God is already doing among the nations. Unity here means aligning ourselves with the wideness of God's mercy.

At the heart of it all is Jesus our Lord, the one who bore the true yoke, fulfilled the law, and poured out grace without distinction. To follow him is to live as people of welcome, humility, and courage, refusing to burden others with what Christ has already carried.

Guiding Truth: The gospel proclaims salvation by grace, calling the church to unity shaped by God's mercy rather than human demands.

Reflection: Where am I tempted to add conditions to the grace of God, for myself or others? How can I practice unity rooted in the Spirit's work rather than cultural or personal preference?

Prayer: God of grace and welcome, keep me from burdening others with what you have already carried. Teach me to seek your Spirit in times of conflict and to walk in unity shaped by mercy. Let my life echo the freedom of your gospel. Amen.

Day 31: Disagreement and the God Who Still Sends

Reading: Acts 15:36–41

After the council at Jerusalem, the church tasted fresh unity and joy. But almost immediately, division arises again, not over doctrine this time, but over people. Paul suggests revisiting the churches they planted to strengthen the believers. Barnabas agrees but insists on bringing John Mark, who had abandoned them on a previous journey. Paul refuses. The text says the disagreement is "sharp." Two companions who had endured persecution together, who had seen miracles and conversions side by side, part ways in conflict.

Barnabas takes Mark and sails to Cyprus. Paul chooses Silas and heads through Syria and Cilicia. The partnership that carried the gospel so far is fractured. There's no resolution offered, no neat ending. Scripture doesn't hide the humanity of the apostles.

And yet, the mission continues. The gospel doesn't stall because of human weakness and differences. Two missionary teams now go out instead of one. The Spirit works through imperfect vessels, even in the midst of their disagreements. Later, Paul will commend both Barnabas and Mark, showing that grace and reconciliation remain possible, even after fracture.

This story is unsettling but also deeply comforting. It shows us that even faithful servants of God disagree, sometimes sharply. Holiness doesn't erase humanity. Discipleship doesn't dissolve difference. The early church wasn't free of tension, and neither are we. But God's mission doesn't depend on our perfection.

When we wrestle with disagreements, conflicts, painful memories, and hurt feelings, Christ Jesus remains present, fulfilling God's divine mission through us, teaching us the way of discipleship, and leading us toward understanding, forgiveness, and healing. I love the way the Scriptures don't hide human frailty but instead show how God works amid our struggles and weaknesses.

This passage invites us into humility. When we experience conflict, the temptation is to demonize the other, to assume we alone see rightly. However, the text offers no clear verdict here: both Paul and Barnabas seek to serve God, and both are used by God. The Spirit is larger than our disagreements, revealing redemption even through our fractures.

This passage speaks prophetically into our polarized and conflicted context. In a time when division seems to fracture communities of faith, when sharp disagreements often escalate into bitterness or separation (over lifestyles, politics, and more), Acts 15 reminds us that brokenness needn't be the end. God's mission is bigger than our conflicts. The Spirit can bring new life even out of our splits.

For our spiritual lives, this story teaches us to hold our conflicts with honesty and grace. It doesn't mean avoiding hard conversations. It doesn't mean pretending sharp disagreements don't exist. It means trusting that God's work doesn't collapse when our relationships do. Christ remains faithful, even when we falter. We'd be silly to think that differences and disagreements won't arise when we're on mission and in fellowship together. This struggle is natural. But God is present, helping us to unite in diversity and mission among differences.

At the center of this story is the one who calls us back together. Jesus prayed that his disciples would be one, and he remains the healer of our divisions. Even when we walk in separate directions, his mercy gathers us into one kingdom, one body, one Spirit.

Guiding Truth: God's mission is greater than our disagreements, and the Spirit can bring fruit even out of division.

Reflection: How do I respond when conflict threatens to divide relationships in faith and mission? Where might God be calling me to trust the Spirit's work, even when reconciliation feels delayed?

Prayer: God of mercy, teach me humility in conflict and hope in division. Use even my weakness for your purposes. Heal what is broken in me and in your church. Keep me trusting that your Spirit still sends, still works, and still redeems. Amen.

Day 32: Unexpected Openings

Reading: Acts 16:1–15

Paul and Silas set out again, and soon Timothy joins them: a young disciple with a Jewish mother and a Greek father, respected by the believers. Paul circumcises him, not because it's required for salvation, but to avoid unnecessary offense as they minister among Jews. This decision, made just after the Jerusalem council declared circumcision unnecessary, shows the complexity of mission. Freedom in Christ doesn't erase sensitivity. Sometimes love requires surrendering rights for the sake of others.

As they travel, the Spirit directs their steps. They try to enter Asia, but the Spirit blocks the way. They turn toward Bithynia, and again the Spirit says no. Closed doors are just as much guidance as open ones. Then, in a vision, Paul sees a man of Macedonia pleading, "Come over to Macedonia and help us." Immediately, they set out, convinced God had called them. Mission unfolds not through human planning but through Spirit-led redirection.

In Philippi, a leading city, they encounter not the Macedonian man of Paul's vision but a group of women gathered for prayer by the river. Among them is Lydia, a dealer in purple cloth, a woman of influence and means. The Lord opens her heart to respond to Paul's message. She and her household are baptized, and she urges the missionaries to stay in her home. Hospitality becomes the foundation of the Philippian church.

This passage shows that mission is relational and adaptive. Paul circumcises Timothy not to preserve tradition but to remove obstacles to the gospel. Faithfulness sometimes means letting go of freedom for the sake of love.

Furthermore, we're reminded that God guides not only through visions of calling but through the frustration of closed doors. Discernment is as much about patience as passion. When our plans falter, it may be the Spirit redirecting us toward unexpected opportunities.

Finally, we should expect the surprising. Paul's vision showed a man, but the first convert in Macedonia was a woman. Lydia, not Paul, becomes the anchor for the new community, her home the first sanctuary. God often begins with the overlooked, subverting expectations, rewriting our strategies, and expanding our imaginations.

Acts 16:1–15 calls us to embrace flexibility, humility, and attentiveness. The Spirit's guidance rarely follows our neat maps. The call of Christ will take us to unforeseen places, among unexpected people, and in surprising ways. And when hearts open, whether in crowded cities or quiet riversides, the kingdom takes root.

At its center, this story points us again to Jesus, who surrendered privilege for love, who trusted the Father's guidance even when it led to the cross, and who welcomed women and men, rich and poor, Jew and Gentile, into one new family. His Spirit still opens hearts, still redirects paths, still births communities in surprising places.

Guiding Truth: God's mission advances through surrendered rights, redirected plans, and unexpected people whose hearts the Spirit opens.

Reflection: Where might God be asking me to surrender a freedom for the sake of love and witness? How can I stay attentive to closed doors as much as open ones, trusting the Spirit's redirection?

Prayer: Spirit of the living Christ, guide my steps. Teach me to yield my freedoms for love, to trust your hand in closed doors, and to welcome the unexpected people you place in my path. Open my heart to your voice and let my home and life become places where your kingdom takes root. Amen.

Day 33: Songs in the Night

Reading: Acts 16:16–40

In Philippi, Paul and Silas meet a slave girl possessed by a spirit of divination. Her enslavers exploit her gift for profit. She follows the apostles for days, crying out that they're servants of the Most High God. Finally, Paul commands the spirit to leave. In an instant, she's free. Unlike her enslavers, who don't care about her and exploit her suffering, the disciples show compassion and mercy, inviting the power of God to bring her the freedom Christ offers. Liberation comes not only to her soul but to her dignity. Yet her freedom enrages her enslavers. Their profit is gone, and in a world that prizes gain over people, freedom is a dangerous commodity.

Paul and Silas are dragged before the authorities, accused of disturbing the city. The crowd joins in, and they're stripped, beaten, and thrown into prison. Their feet are fastened in stocks. At midnight, their bodies bruised, they pray and sing hymns. The other prisoners listen. In the darkness, worship becomes resistance, defiance of despair, a declaration that chains can't bind the gospel.

Suddenly, an earthquake shakes the prison's foundations. Doors fly open. Chains fall loose. Freedom erupts. The jailer, thinking his prisoners have escaped, draws his sword to take his life. But Paul cries out, "Don't harm yourself. We're all here." Grace interrupts violence. Life interrupts despair. Witness to Christ subverts the ways of the world and proclaims another way.

The jailer falls before Paul and Silas, trembling, asking, "What must I do to be saved?" The answer is simple and profound: "Believe in the Lord Jesus, and you'll be saved, you and your household." That night, wounds are washed, bread is shared, and baptismal waters flow. The jailer and his household rejoice, freed not by earthquake alone but by Christ's mercy.

When morning comes, the authorities try to dismiss Paul and Silas quietly. But Paul insists they acknowledge the injustice: they're Roman citizens, unlawfully beaten and imprisoned. The gospel doesn't slip away in silence. It exposes injustice, refusing to let power escape accountability. The magistrates come, apologize, and urge them to leave. The story ends with Paul and Silas visiting Lydia's house, encouraging the believers, then moving on.

This passage names the conflict between the gospel and systems that exploit people for profit. To follow Christ is to confront economic idolatry, where human lives are sacrificed on the altar of gain. Jesus Christ came to free us from spiritual, economic, social, and personal enslavement, offering us the shalom and liberation of God.

Second, it shows the power of worship. In the darkest night, bruised and chained, Paul and Silas sing. Worship becomes protest, hope in the face of despair, light in the midnight hour.

Finally, it calls us to bear witness with both courage and compassion. Paul doesn't flee when the chains fall. He stays, saving the jailer's life and pointing him to Christ. Courage stands firm, but compassion bends low to lift another.

At the center is Jesus, the one who sets captives free, who turns prisons into sanctuaries, and who bears wounds that heal others. His resurrection shakes the foundations of the world and still opens the doors of despair.

Guiding Truth: Worship in the night, liberation in Christ, and courage for justice mark the witness of God's people.

Reflection: Where am I tempted to value profit or comfort over people's dignity and freedom? How can worship in dark seasons become my witness to the hope of Christ?

Prayer: Christ who breaks chains, teach me to sing in the night. Free me from systems that exploit, strengthen me to confront injustice, and give me courage to stay when others need grace. Let my life bear witness to your mercy, power, and unfailing hope. Amen.

Day 34: Turning the World Upside Down

Reading: Acts 17:1–15

In Thessalonica, Paul reasoned in the synagogue for three Sabbaths, opening the Scriptures, showing how the Messiah had to suffer and rise again. The cross isn't a detour, nor a failure; it's the shape of redemption. Some believe. Jews, Greeks, and many influential women join the movement. But not all welcome the news. Jealous leaders incite a mob. They drag Jason and other believers before the authorities, shouting, "These men have turned the world upside down!"

The gospel overturns. It topples idols and unmasks false securities. It refuses to let empire, economy, or piety stand untouched. To proclaim that Jesus is King is to confront every counterfeit throne. No wonder the city trembles. No wonder violence rises. The gospel isn't safe; it's revolution clothed in grace.

In Berea, the story shifts. Here, the Jews are described as "noble." They examine the Scriptures daily to see if Paul's words are valid. Faith grows not in reactionary mobs but in open hearts, attentive to God's word. Many believe. The Spirit stirs where people are willing to listen, to test, to discern.

But opposition is relentless. Agitators from Thessalonica arrive, spreading the same poison of fear and jealousy. Paul is sent away, but Silas and Timothy remain to steady the young community. The word continues to take root, even under pressure.

This passage reveals the truth about the gospel's transformative power. To preach Christ crucified and risen isn't to offer spiritual seasoning for the status quo; it's to announce a kingdom that upends the order of this world. It turns economies shaped by greed into communities of generosity. It turns politics shaped by fear into movements of hope. It turns religion twisted by control into worship rooted in grace.

And yet the gospel also calls us to the patience of Berea. Not all disruption is mob violence. Some upheaval is quiet, born of minds and hearts stretched by Scripture. True revolution is carried by the Spirit breaking open hardened hearts.

For us, this story is a mirror. Do we welcome the unsettling news of Christ's reign, or do we cling to the comfort of old idols? Do we react with jealousy and fear when God works outside our control, or do we open the Scriptures daily, seeking truth with humility and openness?

At the center is Jesus, the one who overturns power not with swords but with wounds, who turns the world upside down by bearing its sin, who reigns not from Caesar's palace but from a cross and an empty tomb. He's still turning things over (our lives, our communities, our idols) so that his kingdom might come.

Guiding Truth: The gospel of Jesus overturns the powers of this world, calling us to courageous disruption and humble openness to God's truth.

Reflection: What idols or systems in my world does the gospel call me to confront or leave behind? Am I willing to be unsettled, to daily search the Scriptures with openness to God's disruptive grace?

Prayer: Christ who turns the world upside down, unsettle my complacency. Strip away the idols I protect. Teach me to follow you with all my mind, heart, and soul. Lead me in your way, truth, and life. Please give me the courage of Thessalonica's accused and the humility of Berea's seekers. Let your kingdom overturn my world until I walk in the new order of grace, justice, and peace. Amen.

Day 35: The Unknown God Made Known

Reading: Acts 17:16–34

Paul walks the streets of Athens, and his spirit burns within him. Everywhere he looks are idols (stone, metal, wood), gods of commerce, gods of philosophy, gods that reflect human ambition more than divine truth. Athens, city of learning, city of debate, city of restless hunger, bows to gods that can't speak.

He's invited to the Areopagus, the hill of power and ideas. There, Paul doesn't flatter. He begins where they are: "I see that in every way you're very religious. As I walked around, I found an altar with this inscription: 'To an unknown god.' What you worship as unknown, I proclaim to you."

The God Paul names isn't contained in shrines or temples. Not served by human hands as though God needed anything. This God gives life and breath to all. This God made the nations, setting their boundaries, so that people might seek and find the One who isn't far from any of us. "In him we live and move and have our being."

Paul proclaims that the time of ignorance is over. God now commands all people everywhere to repent. Why? Because a day of justice is fixed, a day when the world will be judged with equity through the man God has raised from the dead. The resurrection isn't philosophy. It's not a metaphor. It's the guarantee that death and empire have been overturned.

Some sneer. Resurrection is too much, too messy, too embodied. Others are curious: "We want to hear you again." And a few believe: Dionysius, Damaris, and others. Even in the heart of philosophy and idolatry, seeds take root.

This passage is both a mirror and a warning for us. We, too, walk streets lined with idols: screens that demand our attention, markets that measure our worth, politics that promise salvation but deliver chains. We, too, shape gods in our image, gods of success, comfort, and self. The gospel still burns against these lies.

Paul shows us another way: to name the idols, yes, but also to reveal the true God who is Creator, Sustainer, Redeemer. A God not bound by temples or systems, a God who comes near, who breathes life, who raises the crucified. The gospel is both critique and invitation, confrontation and grace.

For our spiritual lives, this passage calls us to discernment. What altars stand in our city, our culture, our hearts, inscribed to "unknown gods"? Where have we traded living faith for lifeless substitutes? And it calls us to witness with courage. We may be mocked. We may be ignored. But the Spirit is already at work, opening hearts like Dionysius and Damaris to believe.

At the center is Jesus, the risen one, the judge of justice, the Lord of life. He's the end of idolatry, the revelation of the unknown, the one in whom we live and move and have our being.

Guiding Truth: The gospel unmasks our idols, calls us to repentance, and reveals the risen Christ as the Lord of life.

Reflection: What idols in my culture or in my own heart still claim devotion that belongs only to God? How can I speak truth with courage in spaces shaped by skepticism, indifference, or idolatry?

Prayer: Living Christ, reveal the idols I cling to. Expose the false gods I worship. Please fill me with your Spirit's fire to name them with courage and to proclaim your resurrection with hope. In you I live, move, and have my being. Please let my whole life bear witness to that truth. Amen.

Day 36: Don't Be Afraid, Keep Speaking

Reading: Acts 18:1–17

Paul arrives in Corinth weary, scarred from rejection, carrying the ache of conflict and the weight of unrelenting opposition. He finds companionship in Aquila and Priscilla, refugees driven from Rome by imperial decree. Together, they work leather and canvas, stitching tents by day and weaving the gospel into hearts by night. The kingdom of God takes root not in palaces but in workshops, among exiles and artisans.

Each Sabbath, Paul reasons in the synagogue, persuading Jews and Greeks. But resistance hardens. Some revile him, spitting words that sting. At that moment, Paul shakes out his garments in protest and declares, "Your blood be on your own heads. I'm innocent. From now on, I'll go to the Gentiles." It's a rupture, a painful break, but also a widening. The gospel isn't chained by rejection; it finds open doors where human boundaries close.

And the next door is literal: the house of Titius Justus, a God-fearer living next to the synagogue. There, the word continues. Even Crispus, the synagogue leader, believes along with his household. Opposition can't halt the Spirit's work; it only shifts its location.

Still, Paul is afraid. Boldness on the outside doesn't erase trembling within. One night, in a vision, the Lord speaks: "Don't be afraid; keep on speaking, don't be silent. For I'm with you, and no one will attack you to harm you, for I have many people in this city." These words steady Paul. He stayed a year and a half, teaching the word of God. Courage isn't the absence of fear but faith clinging to a voice stronger than fear.

Eventually, Paul is dragged before Gallio, the proconsul. The Jews accuse him of persuading people to worship God contrary to the law. However, Gallio dismisses the case, refusing to intervene in matters of theology. Ironically, justice comes not from sympathy but from indifference. Still, Paul is spared. God keeps the promise: "No one will attack you to harm you."

Yet violence erupts anyway, as Sosthenes, the new synagogue leader, is beaten in front of the tribunal. The empire shrugs, unconcerned with injustice unless it disturbs order. This scene names a truth that echoes into our world: power often turns its head while the vulnerable bleed. But the gospel doesn't turn away. It proclaims a kingdom where the bruised are remembered and the silenced find voice.

This passage calls us to three things. First, to courage: "Don't be afraid, keep speaking." Fear is real, but presence is greater: God's presence among us, God's people around us. Second, to wideness: when one door closes, the gospel seeks another. Rejection isn't the end, but often the beginning of a new mission. Third, to solidarity: the kingdom of God takes root among workers, exiles, and the oppressed, not in halls of indifference.

At the center is Jesus, the Word who pitched a tent among us, who faced rejection and violence, who carried fear yet pressed on in obedience. He still says, "Don't be afraid. Keep speaking. I'm with you. I'll never leave you."

Guiding Truth: God's presence steadies our fear, and the gospel continues to speak even when doors close and powers resist.

Reflection: Where am I tempted to silence myself out of fear, forgetting that God's presence is near? How can I expand the reach of the gospel when rejection arises, trusting that new doors will always open?

Prayer: Christ who speaks into my fear, steady my trembling heart. Please teach me to find courage in your presence and resilience in your promises. Let me continue to speak your word of life, stand with the vulnerable, and trust your Spirit to open new doors for your kingdom. Amen.

Day 37: Strengthened in the Way of the Lord

Reading: Acts 18:18–28

After months of labor in Corinth, Paul sets sail again. His journey is weary, marked by vows and farewells, long roads and restless seas. Mission, at its core, is hopeful, sacrificial persistence: faithful steps carried out in the ordinary rhythms of travel and toil. He eventually returns to Antioch, the community that first sent him. The story comes full circle, reminding us that mission is never a solo act. It begins in community, and it returns to community, strengthened and shared.

Meanwhile, the story shifts to Ephesus, where a new figure enters the narrative: Apollos. He's eloquent, learned, and powerful in speech. He knows the Scriptures well and teaches with passion about Jesus. Yet his knowledge is incomplete; he knows only the baptism of John. His zeal outruns his depth.

Here, the courage of Priscilla and Aquila emerges. They don't humiliate Apollos or silence him. They take him aside and explain the way of God more fully. It's discipleship in its purest form: not a contest of egos, but the humble sharpening of one voice by another. Apollos receives their correction, and his ministry deepens. Soon, he becomes a formidable witness, publicly refuting opposition and showing from the Scriptures that Jesus is the Christ.

This passage reminds us that mission is sustained not only by apostles and prophets, but also by ordinary disciples: tentmakers, refugees, teachers, and companions. Priscilla and Aquila aren't in pulpits or councils, yet their faithfulness shapes the church in ways history still remembers.

Second, it shows us that learning in Christ is an ongoing process. Even eloquent Apollos needed guidance. Knowledge alone isn't enough; it must be joined with humility, openness, and correction. The Spirit's work deepens our dependence, teaching us again and again through the voices of others.

Third, it challenges us to discipleship that's both bold and gentle. Priscilla and Aquila embody a wisdom sorely needed: they correct without crushing, they guide without grasping. In a world addicted to public takedowns and humiliation, they choose the hidden way of grace. And through their quiet faithfulness, the church gains a stronger preacher of the gospel.

For our spiritual lives, Acts 18:18–28 calls us to endurance, humility, and community. We endure, like Paul, in the small steps of mission. We remain humble, like Apollos, receiving correction that deepens our witness. We build community, like Priscilla and Aquila, choosing the hidden work of encouragement over the loud performance of pride.

At the center of this story is Jesus, the Way himself. He's the one who calls us deeper, who forms us in community, who strengthens both the eloquent and the ordinary to bear witness. The Spirit is still shaping voices, still refining hearts, still sending disciples into the world: not for their glory, but for the kingdom that turns weakness into strength.

Guiding Truth: The Spirit strengthens the church through humble correction, faithful endurance, and communities rooted in grace.

Reflection: Am I willing to receive correction that deepens my faith, even when it challenges my pride? How might I strengthen others in the way of the Lord with quiet faithfulness rather than public display?

Prayer: Living Christ, keep me humble to learn, faithful to endure, and gentle to strengthen others. Let my words and actions point not to myself but to your truth. Build your church through the hidden faithfulness of ordinary disciples and let your Spirit form us into a people who proclaim your Way with depth and grace. Amen.

Day 38: The Spirit Breaks In

Reading: Acts 19:1–22

Paul arrives in Ephesus and meets disciples who are familiar only with John's baptism of repentance. Their faith is sincere but incomplete. Paul asks, "Did you receive the Holy Spirit when you believed?" They reply, "We haven't even heard that there's a Holy Spirit." So Paul lays hands on them, and the Spirit falls. They speak in tongues and prophesy. Their story reveals that Christianity isn't merely about repentance or moral reform but about receiving the living presence of God.

Paul spends years in Ephesus teaching, persuading, and reasoning. Some resist, but others believe. The gospel grows, not through spectacle alone, but through steady proclamation of truth. Yet signs do accompany the word: extraordinary miracles, healings, and deliverance. The kingdom confronts darkness.

Some Jewish exorcists try to mimic Paul's power, invoking Jesus's name as a formula. But the spirit they confront answers, "Jesus I know, and Paul I recognize, but who are you?" The impostors are beaten and humiliated. The lesson is stark: the name of Jesus isn't magic; it's authority rooted in relationship.

Fear falls on the city. Many confess their sins. Sorcerers burn their scrolls in public, sacrificing wealth for fidelity to Christ. The word of the Lord spreads widely and grows strong.

This passage invites us to examine our own lives. Do we know about Jesus without knowing his Spirit? Do we treat faith as moral reform or as the living presence of God dwelling within us? Do we cling to idols (books, possessions, habits) that need to be burned on the fire of repentance?

At the heart is Jesus, whose name isn't a charm but a living power, whose Spirit fills us, and whose kingdom grows stronger than all counterfeit forces.

Guiding Truth: True faith isn't imitation but Spirit-filled life, burning idols, and spreading the word with power.

Reflection: Do I know the Spirit as presence and power, or only as an idea? What needs to be burned in my life so that Christ alone may reign?

Prayer: Holy Spirit, fill me with life that is real, not imitation. Burn away my idols and counterfeit trusts. Root me in the living Christ, so that my words and deeds proclaim your kingdom with truth and power. Amen.

Day 39: When the Gospel Threatens Idols

Ephesus trembles under the weight of disruption. The gospel doesn't slip quietly into private corners; it confronts the city's heartbeat. A silversmith named Demetrius gathers his guild, men who profit from making shrines of Artemis. He warns that Paul's message (that "gods made with hands aren't gods at all") threatens both their business and the honor of Artemis. Idolatry is rarely just spiritual; it's economic, cultural, and political. To dethrone an idol is to threaten the whole system.

The city erupts into chaos. Crowds seize Paul's companions and rush into the theater, shouting for two hours, "Great is Artemis of the Ephesians!" Their chant echoes the empty fury of idolatry; loud but powerless, fierce but hollow.

The town clerk finally calms the mob, pointing them back to lawful channels. But the truth remains: the gospel has exposed the fragile foundations of their world.

This story reminds us that the kingdom of God isn't a private spirituality. It shakes economies built on exploitation, cultures built on pride, and religions built on fear. The gospel is good news for those experiencing poverty and freedom for those in captivity, but it's bad news for idols that profit from oppression.

For our spiritual lives, this passage asks: what idols shape our city, our culture, our own hearts? What economies and systems depend on lies we would rather not confront? To follow Jesus is to risk uproar, to face hostility when truth exposes false gods.

And yet, the gospel doesn't need mob violence to defend itself. Paul's companions are preserved, not by force, but by God's providence and the rule of law. The gospel isn't fragile. It will outlast Artemis, Rome, empire, and every idol we fashion.

At the center is Jesus, the one greater than all temples, the living presence who confronts and disarms every power. His kingdom can't be shaken, even when mobs rage and idols roar.

Guiding Truth: The gospel unmasks idols, threatening systems of profit and pride, yet its kingdom endures when every false god falls silent.

Reflection: What idols (economic, religious, cultural, political, or personal) does the gospel expose in my world and in my heart? Am I willing to face hostility when truth disrupts the systems around me?

Prayer: Jesus, stronger than every idol, confront the false gods that bind my heart and my world. Please give me the courage to stand in the uproar, trusting that your kingdom can't be shaken. Teach me to live as a witness of your truth and your freedom. Amen.

Day 40: Raised in the Night

Reading: Acts 20:1–12

After riots and turmoil, Paul gathers the disciples, embraces them, and sets out again. His ministry is stitched together by farewells and embraces, departures and tears. The kingdom advances not by empire's might but by the fragile, resilient bonds of love.

He travels through Macedonia and Greece, strengthening the churches. Plots against him force detours: his path is never smooth, yet he doesn't waver. His companions form a diverse company from many cities, evidence that the Spirit is building a church that is wide and deep, not bound by borders.

In Troas, they gather on the first day of the week. The community fills an upstairs room lit by numerous lamps. Paul speaks late into the night: hours stretch, words flow, as if time itself bends under the weight of gospel urgency.

Then a young man named Eutychus, perched on a windowsill, drifts into sleep. He falls three stories, and the room erupts with horror. Life snuffed out in the middle of worship. But Paul rushes down, bends low, embraces the boy, and declares, "Don't be alarmed, for his life is in him." Life returns where death intruded. Grief turns to comfort.

The community eats together, listens still more until dawn, then departs with a testimony: the boy lives. Worship, teaching, death, resurrection, meal: all woven into one long night. It's the gospel enacted in miniature.

This story is strange, but its meaning runs deep. The church is fragile: young disciples fall, faith falters, communities stumble. But in Christ, death isn't the final word. Again and again, life breaks in where we least expect it.

Acts 20:1–12 serves as both a warning and a source of hope. Warning, because discipleship isn't casual: fatigue, distraction, and complacency can lull us into a dangerous sleep. Hope, because even when we fall, Christ bends low, embraces us, and restores life. The kingdom isn't upheld by our stamina but by the Spirit who raises the dead.

At the center is Jesus, who gathered his friends, broke bread with them, entered death, and rose before dawn. The night of Troas echoes the night of the Upper Room and the dawn of resurrection. This is the pattern of our life together: farewell and fellowship, weakness and restoration, cross and resurrection.

Guiding Truth: The church lives not by its strength but by Christ's embrace, who restores life where death intrudes.

Reflection: Where am I tempted to drift into spiritual sleep instead of staying awake to God's presence? How has Christ brought life where I expected only loss?

Prayer: Christ who bends low, keep me awake to your presence. When I fall, lift me with your embrace. Teach me to gather, break bread, and proclaim your life in the night until the dawn of your kingdom comes. Amen.

Day 41: Tears and Warnings

Reading: Acts 20:13–38

Paul calls the Ephesian elders to Miletus for a final farewell. His words aren't polite pleasantries; they're a testament soaked in tears. He reminds them of his example: serving with humility, enduring trials, proclaiming repentance and faith. His ministry wasn't about gain but about giving. His life was poured out in love, not preserved in safety.

He declares the Spirit compels him to go to Jerusalem, not knowing what awaits, except chains and affliction. Yet he doesn't consider his life to be of value to himself. His only aim: to finish the race, to testify to the gospel of grace. His words strip away illusions. The way of Christ isn't self-protection; it's surrender. Not the empire's glory but the cross.

He warns them: fierce wolves will come, distorting truth, preying on the flock. Leadership in the church isn't about prestige; it's about vigilance, sacrifice, and tears. Elders are called not to rule, but to guard; not to exploit, but to protect. He commends them to God and to the word of grace, which builds and sanctifies.

He reminds them he coveted nothing. His hands worked to meet his own needs and to assist those in need. He quotes Jesus: "It's more blessed to give than to receive." The kingdom's economy is generosity, not greed.

When he finishes, they kneel and pray. Tears flow freely. They embrace him, grieved most that they'll never see his face again. The gospel advances not through power, but through love that is willing to weep.

This passage identifies the idols of self-preservation, greed, and control that continue to plague the church. It calls us to a different way: to lay down ambition, to shepherd with tears, to give rather than grasp, to live for the gospel rather than survival.

Acts 20:13–38 calls us to courage and integrity. Courage to walk into unknown suffering with trust in Christ. Integrity to lead not for gain but for the sake of others. Faith that values finishing the race over saving face.

At the center is Jesus: the good shepherd who laid down his life for the flock, who warned of wolves, who gave himself entirely, who prayed with tears, and who now calls us into that same costly love.

Guiding Truth: To follow Christ is to finish the race with courage, tears, and generosity, not clinging to life but giving it away.

Reflection: Where am I tempted to lead or live for gain rather than for service? What would it mean for me to finish my race with joy, even in the face of loss?

Prayer: Good Shepherd, keep me faithful to your call. Please give me the courage to endure, the humility to serve, and the generosity to give. Guard your church from wolves and let my life testify to the gospel of grace until my race is finished in you. Amen.

Day 42: Bound in the Spirit, Bound in Chains

Reading: Acts 21:1–36

The journey to Jerusalem begins with farewells. Paul sails from port to port, embraced by disciples who kneel on beaches and pray through tears. Everywhere he goes, warnings rise: "Don't go up to Jerusalem." Prophets bind their hands with Paul's belt, foretelling the chains awaiting him. Friends plead for him to turn back. Love tries to protect him from suffering.

But Paul is unmoved. "I'm ready not only to be bound, but also to die in Jerusalem for the name of the Lord Jesus." His resolve isn't stubbornness; it's surrender. He walks the path of his Lord, who set his face toward Jerusalem, knowing the cross awaited. Paul won't be deterred. He belongs to Christ, not to safety.

When he arrives, the church leaders welcome him warmly but counsel caution. To quiet rumors, Paul participates in temple rituals. Yet suspicion festers. Some from Asia stir the crowd, accusing him of defiling the holy place. Fury boils. They drag him out, beating him, intent on killing him.

Chaos reigns until Roman soldiers intervene, seizing Paul and binding him with chains. The crowd cries for his death, echoing Jerusalem's mob decades earlier. The pattern repeats: prophetic truth collides with fear, jealousy, and rage. The temple meant for worship becomes a theater of violence.

This passage is a mirror for us. It names the cost of discipleship in a world hostile to truth. The Spirit calls us not to ease but to faithfulness, even when warnings abound, even when friends plead for another path. Paul reminds us that life in Christ isn't something we cling to, but something we give away.

It also unmasks the idols of religion twisted by suspicion and fear. The temple crowd believes they defend holiness, yet they desecrate it with violence. Religion without grace becomes a mob.

At the center is Jesus, the one who entered Jerusalem knowing the cross, who faced mobs and false accusations, who was bound that we might be free. Paul walks in his footsteps, and so must we.

Guiding Truth: To follow Christ is to embrace the Spirit's call, even when it leads into chains and suffering.

Reflection: Where am I tempted to choose safety over obedience to the Spirit's call? How do I discern when fear disguises itself as holiness or wisdom?

Prayer: Christ, who set your face toward Jerusalem, teach me courage. Free me from the grip of safety and anchor me in surrender. Keep me faithful when mobs rage, and let my chains, if they come, become a testimony to your name. Amen.

Day 43: A Testimony in Chains

Reading: Acts 22:1–30

Bound and bruised, Paul addresses the crowd. He speaks in their own language, and a hush falls over the crowd. He tells his story: raised in strict obedience to the law, zealous to the point of violence, persecutor of the Way. Then came the light on the road to Damascus, the voice of Jesus, the blinding glory, the scales falling, the baptism that washed him anew.

Paul's defense isn't an argument but testimony. He doesn't dismantle accusations point by point; he proclaims what Christ has done in him. His life itself becomes the gospel; zeal turned to grace, violence turned to witness.

Yet when he speaks of being sent to the Gentiles, the crowd erupts again. They can tolerate zeal, law, even visions. What they can't abide is a God whose mercy spills beyond their boundaries. The idol exposed isn't irreligion but nationalism. Grace is too wide; the gospel too inclusive.

The Roman commander, confused, prepares to flog Paul for clarity. But Paul claims his citizenship, asserting his rights within the empire. Even in chains, he isn't powerless. He uses the system to protect himself, but his true identity isn't Roman; it's Christ's.

This passage reminds us that testimony is our most powerful witness. Arguments may falter, but no one can deny that a life has been transformed. To follow Christ is to tell the truth of what we were, what Christ has done, and who we're becoming.

It also confronts us with the scandal of grace. Are we willing to follow a God who embraces those we would exclude? Are we ready to let the gospel tear down our boundaries of tribe, class, or nation? The crowd's rage isn't ancient history; it still echoes in our world wherever the wideness of mercy offends our narrowness.

At the center is Jesus, the light on the road, the voice that calls by name, the one who sends us beyond the limits of our imagination. His grace isn't safe, but it's saving.

Guiding Truth: Our truest witness is the story of Christ's transforming grace, a story that shatters boundaries and offends idols of exclusion.

Reflection: What part of my own story is Christ calling me to share as testimony to his grace? Where do I still resist the wideness of God's mercy because it unsettles my boundaries?

Prayer: Light of the world, please remove my pride and open my eyes to your grace. Let my story speak of your mercy and let me not resist the wideness of your love. Make me bold to testify, even in chains, to the Christ who saves and sends. Amen.

Day 44: Christ Stands Near

Reading: Acts 23:1–35

Paul stands before the Sanhedrin, battered but unflinching: "I've fulfilled my duty to God in all good conscience to this day." His words strike a nerve. The high priest orders him struck on the mouth. Paul rebukes him as a "whitewashed wall": exposed as outwardly holy but inwardly corrupt. Religion wielded as violence is hypocrisy.

The council erupts. Pharisees and Sadducees clash over the issue of resurrection. The room descends into chaos, theology turned into a weapon, truth drowned out by shouting. Soldiers pull out Paul before he's torn apart.

That night, alone in the fortress, the Lord stands near. Not far. Near. "Take courage! As you've testified about me in Jerusalem, so you must also testify in Rome." Chains don't silence Paul. Violence doesn't end his mission. The presence of Christ is his assurance.

Meanwhile, a conspiracy forms: more than forty men swear an oath not to eat or drink until Paul is dead. But their secrecy is pierced by providence. Paul's nephew overhears, warns the tribune, and Roman soldiers escort Paul with overwhelming force: four-hundred-and-seventy men guarding one prisoner. God's purposes aren't thwarted.

Paul is sent to Caesarea and delivered to the governor Felix. What seemed like defeat becomes a bridge to Rome. The Lord's word proves true.

This passage names the hypocrisy of religion twisted into violence, calling us to repent of every system that cloaks cruelty in holiness. It warns us that truth often divides, that the gospel will unsettle even the most pious chambers.

But above all, it consoles us with the nearness of Christ. In the night of fear and loneliness, he stands near. His presence is our courage, his promise our future.

Guiding Truth: When religion fails and enemies conspire, Christ stands near, turning chains into pathways for witness.

Reflection: How have I seen Christ's nearness in times of fear or rejection? Where am I called to trust that what looks like defeat may be God's path to witness?

Prayer: Christ who stands near, steady me when the world rages. Unmask hypocrisy, protect me from fear, and turn my chains into testimony. Let my courage rest not in myself but in your faithful presence. Amen.

Day 45: Faithfulness Before Power

Reading: Acts 24:1–27

Paul stands trial before Felix. The high priest arrives with a lawyer, Tertullus, whose flattery fills the court: "We enjoy great peace under your foresight." Lies of loyalty cloak accusations of rebellion. Empire always prefers flattery to truth.

Paul speaks plainly. He doesn't flatter or grovel. He affirms his worship of the God of his ancestors, his belief in resurrection, and his striving to keep a clear conscience before God and people. His defense isn't a strategy; it's testimony. He belongs to Christ, not to the tribunal.

Felix postpones judgment, feigning caution. He listens to Paul speak about faith in Christ Jesus, about righteousness, self-control, and the coming judgment. Felix trembles. Yet he delays, hoping for a bribe. Power is moved but not transformed, convicted but not converted.

Paul remains in prison for two years, forgotten by politics but not by God. The word doesn't falter, even when its messenger is bound.

This story exposes idols of power and corruption. Felix trembles at the truth but clings to greed. He mirrors our own temptations: to admire righteousness but refuse repentance, to feel conviction yet postpone obedience. The gospel confronts every seat of power, not with flattery but with courage, not with bribes but with truth.

For us, Paul's witness is a model of faithfulness. We may never stand before governors, but we're daily called to speak truth without compromise, to live with integrity even when silenced, and to trust that God's kingdom advances in ways unseen.

At the center is Jesus, who stood silent before Pilate, who bore injustice with courage, and who embodies righteousness, self-control, and judgment in perfect harmony. His presence strengthens us when we stand before the powers of our day.

Guiding Truth: Faithfulness means speaking truth without compromise, even when power delays, resists, or seeks to corrupt.

Reflection: Where am I tempted to postpone obedience, like Felix, trembling yet delaying? How can I embody courage and integrity when faced with systems that prefer flattery or compromise?

Prayer God of truth, give me courage to speak faithfully, even before powers that resist. Keep me from delay and compromise. Let my life witness to your righteousness and kingdom, trusting that your purposes endure even in long seasons of silence. Amen.

Day 46: Appealing to the True Judge

Reading: Acts 25:1–22

Two years have passed, and Paul remains a prisoner. A new governor, Festus, takes office. Almost immediately, the Jewish leaders press their case against Paul, asking Festus to bring him to Jerusalem. Beneath the veneer of legal procedure lies a darker plan: they're plotting an ambush to kill him. Religious fervor cloaks violence: hidden agendas manipulate justice.

Festus refuses the request but invites them to make their accusations in Caesarea. When they arrive, they hurl charges they can't prove. Paul defends himself with clarity: "I've done nothing wrong against the law of the Jews or against the temple or against Caesar." His innocence echoes Jesus's trial years earlier: accusations multiplied, evidence absent, truth silenced by envy.

Festus, seeking favor with the leaders, asks Paul if he is willing to stand trial in Jerusalem. Paul, discerning the trap, appeals to Caesar. His words are bold: "I stand at Caesar's tribunal, where I ought to be tried. If I'm guilty, I don't refuse to die. But if their charges are false, no one has the right to hand me over. I appeal to Caesar!"

The room shifts. Festus confers with his council, then grants the appeal. Paul's fate is no longer local; it's tied to Rome itself. What appears to be entrapment becomes the path to the very heart of the empire. The gospel is carried forward through injustice into the halls of power.

Later, King Agrippa and Bernice arrive in Caesarea. Festus consults them, admitting his perplexity: he has a prisoner with no clear charges, only disputes over religious questions and "a certain Jesus, who was dead but whom Paul claims is alive." The governor of Rome stumbles over the very heart of the gospel. The resurrection sounds like nonsense to him, yet it remains the hinge of history, the claim that refuses to be silenced.

This passage names realities we still face. Systems of power often bend the rules of justice to maintain influence. Leaders prefer compromise over truth, favoring fairness over justice. Religion can cloak violence. Yet through it all, God works. Paul's chains become the channel by which the gospel moves toward Rome. What appears to be failure may be providence in disguise.

For our lives, this story asks: Where do we place our ultimate appeal? Not in corrupt systems or fragile leaders but in the true Judge, the living Christ. Like Paul, we're called to courage: to stand firm, to speak truth, to entrust our lives to God's higher court even when human courts falter.

At the center is Jesus, the one falsely accused, unjustly condemned, yet vindicated by resurrection. He is the Judge who hears every appeal, the King before whom every power will bow.

Guiding Truth: When earthly systems bend justice, we appeal to the risen Christ, the true Judge who vindicates and advances his mission.

Reflection: Where am I tempted to place my hope in human systems of justice rather than in Christ's kingdom? How might my trials become pathways for the gospel's advance?

Prayer: Risen Christ, my true Judge, steady me when false accusations rise and justice bends. Teach me to stand firm in truth, to entrust my life to your verdict, and to see my chains as channels of your mission. Amen.

Day 47: Testifying Before Kings

Reading: Acts 25:23–26:32

The scene is drenched in spectacle. King Agrippa and Bernice enter the great hall with pomp: robes glimmering, soldiers gleaming, and power parading itself. Festus presides, politicians gather, courtiers attend. And in the center stands Paul: chained, scarred, weary, and unafraid. The contrast couldn't be sharper: the empire's grandeur against the humble witness of a prisoner who carries eternity in his heart.

Festus introduces Paul with bemusement, confessing that he has no real charge to send to Caesar. What troubles him is "a certain Jesus, who was dead, but whom Paul claims is alive." The entire machinery of Rome is puzzled by resurrection. Power understands violence, wealth, and fear, but not life rising from death.

Paul begins to speak not as a defendant but as a herald. He stretches out his hand and tells his story again. The persecutor turned apostle. The light that blinded him on the Damascus road. The voice that called his name: "Saul, Saul, why do you persecute me?" The mercy that turned his zeal into mission. He recounts the commission: "I'm sending you to open their eyes, to turn them from darkness to light, from the power of Satan to God, that they may receive forgiveness of sins and a place among the sanctified."

This isn't a legal defense; it's testimony before thrones. Paul's words pierce the opulent hall like prophecy. He proclaims that Christ's suffering and resurrection fulfill what the prophets foretold, that light has come not only for Israel but for the nations. The gospel is public truth, not private religion.

Festus interrupts, his voice echoing through marble: "You're out of your mind, Paul! Too much learning has driven you insane!" But Paul stands firm: "I'm not insane, most excellent Festus. What I'm saying is true and reasonable." Truth sounds like madness to power that can't imagine a kingdom without coercion.

Paul turns to Agrippa: "Do you believe the prophets? I know that you do." Agrippa hesitates, deflecting: "Do you think you can persuade me to be a Christian so quickly?" The air is thick with irony: kings evading the truth spoken by a chained man. Yet Paul's response is fearless and tender: "Short time or long, I pray that not only you but all who are listening may become what I am, except for these chains."

This is the heart of witness. Paul's faith isn't defensive, bitter, or ashamed. He's hopeful, inviting, and gracious in his defiance. The prisoner blesses his captors. The bound one offers freedom.

When the assembly disperses, Agrippa admits the truth: "This man could've been set free if he hadn't appealed to Caesar." Yet Paul's freedom is already secure. He's bound to Christ, not to Rome. The gospel will reach Caesar's court, not by strategy but by suffering.

This passage invites us to courage. We can speak truth before power, knowing that resurrection confounds empires, and bear witness with gentleness and conviction, believing that even palaces aren't beyond the reach of grace.

At the center stands Jesus: the one before whom all rulers will one day stand, who overturned death itself, and who empowers his people to speak truth, even in chains.

Guiding Truth: The gospel confounds the powerful, revealing a kingdom where truth speaks through chains and resurrection dismantles every empire's claim.

Reflection: When have I felt called to speak truth in places of power, fear, or indifference? How might I bear witness with both courage and compassion, trusting that resurrection still unsettles the world's thrones?

Prayer: Christ, before whom every throne will bow, give me courage to speak truth with grace. When power mocks or misunderstands, let resurrection shape my hope. Make my life a testimony to your kingdom and a freedom that no chain can bind. Amen.

Day 48: Storms, Sovereignty, and the Slow Work of Trust

Reading: Acts 27:1–26

Paul sets sail for Rome under guard, a prisoner carried by the empire's machinery. The sea glimmers with promise, but the winds proclaim a warning. Luke writes with the precision of one who remembers every shudder of the ship, every crack of rope, every wave that rose against them. It's a parable of faith in a world that worships control.

The centurion, Julius, treats Paul kindly at first. However, soon decisions are made based on convenience. The pilot and the ship's owner urge pressing on despite Paul's warning: "I perceive that this voyage will end in disaster and much loss." The voice of caution, born of discernment, is overruled by profit and pride. Our world often has no patience for slowness, no ears for prophets.

Then the wind turns violent. The ship is caught in a tempest so fierce it earns a name: Euraquilo, the northeast wind. The crew lashes ropes around the hull, jettisons cargo, and surrenders to the storm. Days blur. The sun and stars disappear. They stop eating. Hope drains from them like water through the planks.

And then, amid the howling wind, Paul speaks again, not as a prisoner, but as a prophet. "You should have listened to me," he says, not with arrogance but with gravity. Yet his words turn from warning to grace: 'Take courage! Not one of you will perish. Only the ship will be lost."

He tells them of an angel's visitation in the night: "Don't be afraid, Paul. You must stand before Caesar. And behold, God has granted you all those who sail with you." Paul believes. The prisoner becomes the steady center of the storm.

This is a story for our own age: an age that sails ahead despite warning, driven by profit, progress, and pride. We trade discernment for speed, wisdom for ambition, holiness for efficiency. We think we can outmaneuver the wind. But eventually, storms reveal what empires forget: control is an illusion, and the sea belongs to God.

Yet even in judgment, grace moves. God doesn't abandon the reckless sailors or the unbelieving centurion. Because Paul is on board (because a person of faith still prays and listens), mercy spreads across the ship. The presence of one who trusts God becomes the vessel of salvation for many who don't yet believe.

Acts 27 reminds us that faith is an anchor in the midst of storms. To belong to Christ is to trust that no storm can steal the purpose God has spoken over us.

At the heart of this story is Jesus: the Lord of wind and wave, who once slept in the boat while his disciples panicked. His calm presence still speaks through the Pauls of every generation: "Take courage. You won't be lost. The ship may break, but my promise won't."

Guiding Truth: Faith anchors us when control collapses; even in the storm, God's promise stands, and grace extends through those who trust.

Reflection: Where am I trying to outrun the storm instead of trusting God's presence within it? How might my faith, like Paul's, become an anchor of mercy for those around me?

Prayer: Lord of wind and wave, steady me when I am tossed by fear. Strip me of illusions of control and teach me to trust your promise in the storm. When life is out of control, and all my misconceptions of power and control are gone, lead me to a deeper trust in you. Let my faith become a shelter for others until your dawn breaks over the chaos. Amen.

Day 49: Shipwrecks and Strange Kindness

Reading: Acts 27:27–28:10

Fourteen nights at sea. Fourteen nights of chaos, hunger, fear, and exhaustion. The sailors (once confident masters of their craft) now drift helplessly, driven by a storm that won't relent. The waves mock their skill, and the darkness feels endless.

Then, in the black hours before dawn, they sense land. Panic and hope collide. They drop anchors and pray for light. Some try to flee in lifeboats, grasping at self-preservation. Paul stops them: "Unless you stay with the ship, you can't be saved." His words cut through the panic. Survival, paradoxically, depends on surrender: on staying rather than fleeing.

At daybreak, he urges them to eat: "You need strength to survive." He breaks bread, gives thanks, and shares it with all 276 souls aboard. Eucharist in the storm. Communion among pagans and prisoners. Gratitude in the wreckage. The act is almost defiant: thanksgiving before deliverance.

Then comes the crash. The ship splinters against a sandbar; the hull tears open; chaos returns. Soldiers prepare to kill the prisoners to prevent escape, but the centurion, protecting Paul, orders otherwise. All leap into the sea. Some swim. Some cling to planks. All reach the shore alive. What Paul had promised has come to pass: not one is lost.

They crawl onto the island of Malta, drenched and shivering, only to encounter unexpected grace. The locals (called "barbarians" by Luke, meaning simply outsiders) show unusual kindness. They build a fire. They welcome the survivors without suspicion. Civilization, it seems, doesn't always dwell where empire says it does. Sometimes compassion burns brightest on the margins.

As Paul gathers wood for the fire, a viper strikes his hand. The locals wait for divine retribution, expecting him to swell and die. But he shakes off the serpent into the flames and suffers no harm. Fear turns to awe; judgment gives way to wonder.

Soon, Paul is healing the sick. He lays hands on Publius's father, stricken with fever, and the man is restored. Others come (people from the island, bringing their pain, their hope) and Paul heals them too. Grace flows outward from the wreck, from the survivor who still believes that every breath, every island, every stranger, belongs to God's story.

This passage exposes a truth our world resists: that salvation often arrives through shipwreck. Control must shatter before grace can lead us ashore. And sometimes, the kindness we fear we'll never find waits in the hands of strangers we once despised.

For us, Malta is wherever we find ourselves washed up after disaster: half-drowned, emptied of illusions, yet met by mercy that surprises us. There, Christ meets us in the fire, in the hands of strangers, in the healing that follows loss.

At the center is Jesus, the shipwrecked Savior who bore our storms, was cast among the wreckage of the world, and rose to heal those who thought him cursed. His resurrection is Malta for the soul: an island of mercy after the world has broken apart.

Guiding Truth: Grace meets us in the wreckage, and God's healing flows through those who trust love more than fear, even among strangers and storms.

Reflection: What storms or shipwrecks have stripped away my illusion of control, leaving room for grace? Who are the "strangers" through whom God might be showing unexpected kindness?

Prayer: Christ of the wreck and the shore, meet me in the ruins of my control. Teach me to stay when I want to flee, to give thanks before deliverance, and to welcome the kindness of strangers. Let my scars become channels of healing for others. Amen.

Day 50: Unhindered

Reading: Acts 28:11–31

The journey that began in chains ends in a rented house. Paul finally reaches Rome: not in triumph, but through shipwreck, trial, and mercy. The empire's heart is before him, the power that shaped the world and crucified his Lord. Yet Luke's final words aren't about Caesar or empire. They're about the gospel: "He proclaimed the kingdom of God and taught about the Lord Jesus Christ with all boldness and without hindrance."

That last phrase ("without hindrance") is defiant. Paul is still under guard, still confined, still watched by the empire. But the Word of God isn't chained. The gospel keeps moving through the cracks of prisons and politics, flowing where control can't reach.

When Paul gathers the Jewish leaders in Rome, he doesn't accuse or resent. He testifies. He tells the story of hope: the story of Israel fulfilled in Jesus. Some believe. Others reject. The ancient tension continues. Paul quotes the prophet Isaiah: "You will be ever hearing but never understanding." His tone isn't bitter but brokenhearted. Truth has come near, yet many still refuse to see.

However, Luke's narrative doesn't end with rejection; it concludes with a mission. Paul remains open, welcoming all who come to him. The apostle of the nations becomes a host in captivity. Hospitality becomes resistance. The empire surrounds him with guards, but he surrounds the empire with grace.

It's a quiet, subversive ending. No courtroom drama. No martyrdom scene. Just a prisoner teaching, welcoming, praying, and proclaiming the kingdom of God. The gospel doesn't need spectacle to win; it requires faithfulness.

Acts 28 invites deep reflection on what "unhindered" really means. It's not about freedom from circumstance. It's about freedom within circumstance: the kind of inner liberty that no regime, illness, or fear can silence. Paul's boldness doesn't come from status or success but from abiding in the Spirit. He's not angry at what has been denied him; he's alive to what grace still makes possible.

The book of Acts ends open-ended because the mission continues. The Spirit still writes new chapters through every person who refuses despair, who welcomes others in the midst of limitation, who embodies good news where empire and cynicism reign. Every act of mercy, every word of truth, every quiet defiance of despair adds another line to Luke's unfinished story.

Our world is still Rome: powerful, anxious, enthralled by wealth and fear. And yet the gospel still moves through prisons, protests, sanctuaries, and kitchens. Through those who pray, speak truth, and live love "without hindrance."

The final image isn't of a man in chains, but of a kingdom unbound. Christ reigns not from a throne of gold but from the hearts of the faithful: the same Christ who walks through our own Rome, calling us to bear witness with joy, patience, and courage.

Guiding Truth: The Spirit of God can't be silenced; even in confinement, the gospel moves freely through those who live and speak with courage and love.

Reflection: Where in my life might God be inviting me to live "unhindered," even in limitation? How can my home, work, or struggle become a place of welcome and witness?

Prayer: Spirit of freedom, move through the locked doors of my fear. Let my limitations become the ground of your grace. Teach me to live and speak the gospel without hindrance: to love boldly, welcome freely, and trust your kingdom to keep advancing. Amen.

Appendix 1: Would You Help?

Writing a book takes immense effort. It's a sustained labor of love over months, even years. Every page carries hours of thought, prayer, revision, and hope. And while the writing may be solitary, the life of a book is communal. That's where you come in. If this book has meant something to you, I'd be deeply grateful if you could help it find its way into more hands and hearts.

There are two simple but powerful ways you can do that.

First, consider leaving a short review on Amazon (and Goodreads would be wonderful too). Even just a few sentences can help others discover the book, as reviews significantly influence how books are recommended and shared online. You can do that by visiting Amazon or searching for this book and writing a review. Even a short note helps people find the book.

Second, if the book has stirred something in you, would you share it with others: friends, groups, churches, or anyone who might benefit from its message?

Your support helps keep this work going, and it means more than I can say. Thank you for being part of this journey.

Find this book on these pages:

1. Amazon:

https://www.amazon.com.au/stores/author/B008NI4ORQ

2. Goodreads:

https://www.goodreads.com/author/show/20347171.Graham_Joseph _Hill

3. Author Website:

https://grahamjosephhill.com/books/

Appendix 2: About Me

Graham Joseph Hill (OAM, PhD) is an Adjunct Research Fellow and Associate Professor at Charles Sturt University, and one of Australia's most prolific and awarded Christian authors. He's written more than twenty books, including Salt, Light, and a City, which was named Jesus Creed's 2012 Book of the Year (church category); Healing Our Broken Humanity (with Grace Ji-Sun Kim), named Outreach Magazine's 2019 Resource of the Year (culture category); and World Christianity, shortlisted for the 2025 Australian Christian Book of the Year. In 2024, Graham was awarded the Medal of the Order of Australia (OAM) for his service to theological education. He lives in Sydney with his wife, Shyn.

Author and Ministry Websites

GrahamJosephHill.com

GrahamJosephHill.Substack.com

youtube.com/@GrahamJosephHill_Author

Linktr.ee/dailydevotions

facebook.com/grahamjosephhill/

instagram.com/grahamjosephhill/

amazon.com.au/stores/author/B008NI4ORQ

goodreads.com/author/show/20347171.Graham_Joseph_Hill

Books

See all my books at GrahamJosephHill.com/books

Appendix 3: Connect With Me

I'd love to stay connected with you. You can sign up to my Substack, Spirituality and Society with Hilly, where I share new writing, spiritual reflections, and updates on future books. Please find me on Substack: https://grahamjosephhill.substack.com

You can also find my books on my website: https://grahamjosephhill.com/books

You can also connect with me through my Facebook author page: https://www.facebook.com/GrahamJosephHill/

www.ingramcontent.com/pod-product-compliance
Lightning Source LLC
Chambersburg PA
CBHW031514040426

42445CB00009B/231